T0286148

THE IDEAL COMMUNIST CITY

Translated from the Italian text (Idee per la Città Communista)
il Saggiatore, Milano, 1968.

For information, address:

i press incorporated
145 Hanover Street
Boston, Massachusetts 02108

George Braziller, Inc.
1 Park Avenue
New York, New York 10016

Library of Congress Catalog Card Number: 75-129358
Standard Book Number: Clothbound—0-8076-0576-X
                                  Paperbound—0-8076-0575-1

First printing.

THE IDEAL
COMMUNIST CITY

By
Alexei Gutnov
A. Baburov
G. Djumenton
S. Kharitonova
I. Lezava
S. Sadovskij
of Moscow University

Translated by RENEE NEU WATKINS

i press series on the human environment

GEORGE BRAZILLER · NEW YORK

CONTENTS

This book was initiated by the architecture faculty of the University of Moscow in the late fifties. For the Italian edition in 1968 the material was enlarged and revised by the authors, a group of young urbanists, architects, and sociologists, who represent a renewal of ideas and men that is taking place in Soviet Russia, especially in fields concerned with the organization of the physical environment. Their work is particularly original in its general assumptions, method of inquiry, and choice of models. The authors turn away from the proposition that the city should attempt to restore the habits and appearance of the countryside. This proposition adapted from the bourgeois naturalism of the nineteenth century, contradicted the ideological foundations of communism. By contrast, what is proposed in this book is world-wide urbanization. The authors' design concept, the New Unit of Settlement, incorporates countryside with city, conceiving both as a communication network, uniformly intense and diffused.

The method by which this original proposition is applied is as new as the proposition itself. No longer relying upon academic preconceptions, the authors have based their architectural and urban proposals on the analysis of life in the existing Soviet society and the directions of change within it. While the models and formal solutions are only sketched and presented hypothetically, they build upon the rich heritage left by Soviet architecture and urbanism in the twenties. Unlike Western architectural "revivals," which consistently turn toward the past and are pseudo-innovative, the Soviet heritage suggests the idea of a "revolutionary tradition" to serve as an example for future-oriented planning.

Milan, Italy, May 1970

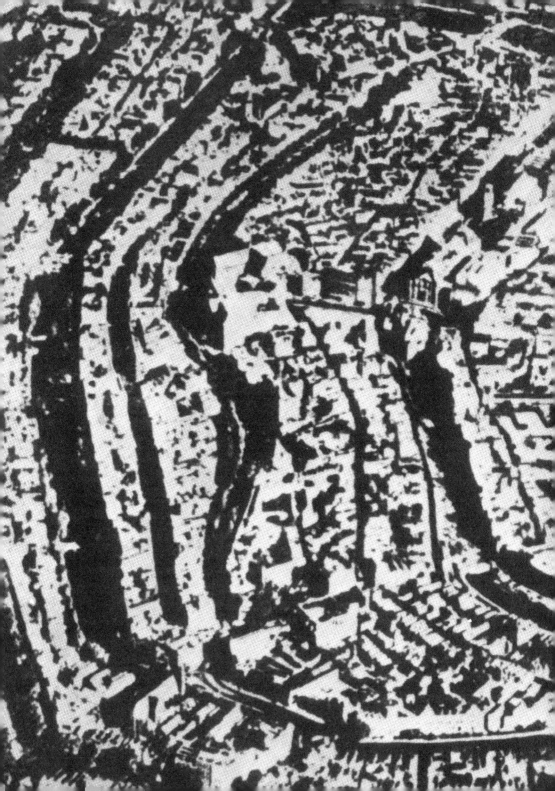

TODAY AND TOMORROW

Today the city does not fulfill its essential purpose, which is to be an organic community.

Seeking new approaches, architecture strives to create the city of the future.

We must find a structure that responds organically to the social and economic functions of the new urban life.

We must understand how architecture will be transformed by the new functional structure of urban environments.

The architect's creative powers turn to the future.

All that is being built today in our country is being incorporated into the material substructure of communist society. It is the function of planning to calculate the immediate needs of the future. However, the vision that seems to provide a firm basis on which to construct a housing project or a city may prove to fall short in the end, or to be in some ways irrelevant. It is impossible to predict accurately the development that will take place several years from now. Time will inevitably show the limitations of today's solutions.

Fundamental changes in the structure of the urban environment can, however, be anticipated. Planning must take such changes into account, and tomorrow should not be sacrificed to an imagined expediency of the moment.

Examination of the errors of the past can help us to define our problem correctly, yet even the best job of criticism cannot do away with the problem. It must, in some positive sense, be solved.

Seeking new approaches in architecture, conscious of its growing possibilities, we look first of all at the city.

The city embodies the highest achievements of our material and spiritual culture. As an inclusive organization, it connects residence and factory, past and future, individual and society.

But the contemporary city is a tangle of contradictions, partly because of the complexity of its economic and social parts, and partly because its earlier development came about through accidental historical processes. In the Soviet Union, in contrast to capitalist countries, urban construction is being

The City Is a Tangle of Contradictions

Areas of intensive industrial development

key:
△ new cities
○ large zones of new development
□ zones of older development

Peterborough ○   Norwich □

Northampton ○
□ Bedford   Ipswich ○
Banbury □ △ Bletchley
                              Stansted □ Colchester
Aylesbury □   ○ □

                         Chelmsford
Swindon ○   Reading   □ Southend
Newbury △ □   □ Medway towns
                    Maidstone □
                              Ashford
                              ○

Southampton △
Poole □   Portsmouth   □ Hastings

undertaken as part of a unified plan for the national economy. Our urban planning, however, has not yet been able wholly to overcome the accidental character of city growth.

Intensive industrial development often brings irreversible changes in the functional structure of the environment, including a confusion of industrial and residential areas and the lack of a well-defined traffic system. Old city plans prove incapable of assimilating a continuous influx of population.

City planning to date has not given enough consideration to incessant growth as a continuing factor in the development of cities. This omission alone is ample proof that present theoretical thought in the fields of building and planning is inadequate to direct a communist building program.

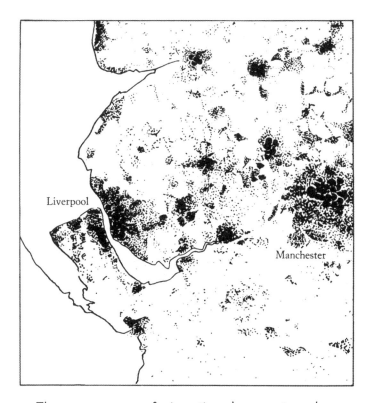

Liverpool

Manchester

The appearance of gigantic urban centers, human agglomerations of every sort, is not a matter of chance. The development of socialist production requires, and will continue to require, the creation of new and ever more massive territorial-industrial complexes; it is bound to regroup vast populations at selected geographical points.

In our pursuit of a congruent structure, we must make sure that the one we define corresponds organically to the social and economic functioning of the new urban world. This functional structure should be a matrix or, to be precise, a social program for architects and city planners as organizers of social process in time and space. As a model, this structure must meet all the basic needs of any urban environment or city, regardless of the specific features of the situa-

7

1. Years from 1800 on. By 2,000 the urbanized population will constitute 75% of the total population of the globe.
   1. Rural areas—pop. below 5,000
   2. Towns—pop. between 5,000 and 20,000
   3. Cities—pop. between 20,000 and 100,000
   4. Cities—pop. above 100,000
2. Years from 1800 on. The growth of urbanized population in the U.S.S.R. was considerably greater than the growth of its total population.
   1. Growth of urbanized pop., U.S.S.R.
   2. Growth of total pop., U.S.S.R.

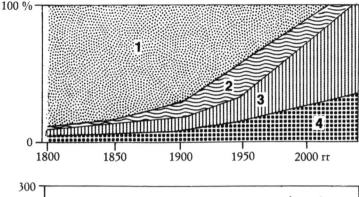

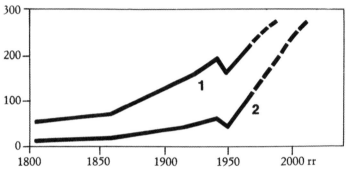

tion and regardless of the creativity of the individual architect. Today, given automobile traffic and consumer services, the planned microsector represents the ultimate modernization of the residential city block. The microsector, however, as a basic structural unit for contemporary residential areas does not satisfy all the complex social, economic, and technical needs involved. The result: bad conditions of health and sanitation, traffic frustrations, a great waste of time, and the isolation of individuals in extremely confined spaces.

Social Relationship What should be the relation of urban environments to nature? To production? What expressive means are legitimate in designing them, etc.?

These are questions that arise for anyone who tries to establish criteria in order to evaluate particular architectural proposals. We need to understand the evolutionary direction that determines specific types of construction, changes in the city's elements, and reorganization of the different sectors of building activity. Otherwise we cannot analyze results or find direction within each field of creative endeavor.

The scope of this inquiry can now be defined: after establishing a scientific projection of the model of communist life, which by agreement guides all the activities of our people, and after examining actual contemporary trends in urbanization and relocation of population, we shall attempt to outline the functional structure of an urban environment that is communist in character and show how this new functional structure determines methods of three-dimensional composition and expressive possibilities in architecture.

SOCIAL RELATIONSHIPS AND THE

URBAN ENVIRONMENT

To resolve the problem of the city scientifically we must begin by studying life in the society, that is, the sum of relationships and wider associations shaping all social experience in time and space.

A logical analysis of sociological models shows that the economic system, through its impact upon all levels of social relationship, determines the urban form of a given society.

The creative relationship with its spectrum of sociological elements is the dominant feature of a society, and it determines classless communist group structure.

What should be our criteria for analyzing the functional structure of the communist city?

First of all, we must arrive at one basic relationship that can express the whole social process (economic, esthetic, creative, etc.) and that can serve as an objective standard for measuring. We must examine the diverse forms of this relationship in different social contexts. Then we can construct a general functional model of the social organism that can be applied accurately to the historical analysis of any particular urban settlement. Accordingly, we shall be able to see the influence of different social systems on the same spatiotemporal organization and to foresee future trends.

All this preliminary work is necessary if we are to go beyond mere wishful thinking in trying to resolve the problem of the communist city. Considering its chief activities and basic social units with due care, we must also define and clarify the goals characteristic of communist society. Before we can think about a single housing plan, we need objective data on the principal types of structure to be created and the functions and relationships of the social groups to be housed. The distribution and ordering of the total population can be studied only on the basis of facts, with a knowledge of the types of structure required and their interrelationship (quantity of each type, sizes of groups to be housed in communist society, limits on size of residential areas, distances between such areas, dynamics and discontinuity of the urbanization process).

Social Relationship

Soviet Relationships in the Soviet World

To understand how social relationships manifest themselves in spatial and temporal organization we need a materialist approach and clear basic premises.

Marx and Engels, in creating the materialist concept of society, gave their views a scientific basis. They stated: "Our basic premises are not arbitrary assumptions or dogmas but concrete facts, from which one can abstract only by an act of imagination. . . . These can be established empirically."[1]

The premises in question concern human beings, each with a specific biological make-up. They include their need for food, clothing, shelter, etc., the context into which they are born (natural and social), and finally their own vital activity, which takes two different forms: the natural—birth, growth, and reproduction—and the social—the collaboration of many individuals in a system of common action to ensure survival.

"In this way men enter into material relationships with each other, relationships conditioned both by their needs and by the means of production, relationships as old as man himself. It is these relationships assuming ever new forms which make up what we mean by 'history.' "[2]

Those material and social bonds that men share in common and the many-faceted interdependence of human relationships, as distinct from man's personal confrontation with nature and his own vital processes, were viewed by Marx and Engels as social relationships. All these, including relationships founded on language and thought, were viewed as aspects of a single process and, in a broad sense, as aspects of the total human experience (for the social process itself is also conditioned by the structure of the human body and its environment).

The Marxist conception of social relations together

[1] Karl Marx and Friedrich Engels, **Socinenija**, Vol. III, p. 18.
[2] **Ibid.**, pp. 28–29.

with the recent achievements of certain sciences—
cybernetics, information theory, human engineering,
and the esthetics of technology—not only enable us
to gain a picture of demography and population
movements (the latter with the help of statistics) but
also to shape and control social processes.

The achievements of these sciences make it possible
to study social relationships as occurrences in the
process of information exchange. It becomes possible
to compute the interaction of all the internal and
external factors that maintain the social process in
its normal condition. We can view social relationships
as sets of material interactions existing in time and

space, taking place among individuals, and can apply objective and quantitative measurement to any desired social process.

The effectiveness of this approach was first proved in the application of time-motion studies to airplane pilots, automobile drivers, and the routines of men in control rooms. Instrument panels, instruments, and steering devices were constructed to correspond perfectly to the physiological and psychological capacities of the man and his working posture. The idea that the quantitative and qualitative character of a space—its dimensions, form, color, light, temperature, etc.—as well as time and change plays an enormous role in production and greatly affects the vital morale of the individual worker is one that is gaining influence in every sector of human activity.

We have learned to give up methods for planning machines, articles of consumption, and living spaces because they failed to allow for the physiological and psychological peculiarities of the human organism and its cultural needs. Human engineering has now spread to every area of life.

In interior design we no longer think so much in terms of furnishings as in terms of creating an environment precisely suited to the functions to be performed. The same basic attitude is coming to be accepted in exterior architecture. However, in most cases the scientific organization of space and time, based on the objective measurement of social realities, still has not become the basis of planning.

Scientific research into social reality has become possible today and is of undeniable importance for the solution of urban problems.

Use of an Analytical Model of Social Relationships

18

Any social function can be analyzed as one or a combination of several social relationships that are possible under given conditions. As seen in a model of social interaction, the conditions define and shape a particular function and indicate the quantitative and qualitative characteristics of the participants and the environment.

By using models based on analysis of social relationships we are able to describe the essential formative stages of individual life. Levels of mental and physical maturity can be defined in terms of the social behavior that is characteristic at various stages of growth in a given society.

The life of a man from cradle to grave, including both his labor and the raising of children, can be seen as a unique system of interactions between a set of basic biological facts and a combination of natural and social relationships (all manifested in the context of a culture and shaped by it). We can construct a general human model consistent with the anatomy of society as a whole, logically derived from prototypal relationships, and including all the functions essential to any individual life regardless of its particular culture.

The following steps mark the formative stages of personality:

1. Relationship of mother and infant: a stage in which the genotype or hereditary features unfold and in which the foundations are laid for social thresholds of perception.

2. Relationship with parents: a stage at which different social relationships begin to be distinguished and language is formed.

3. Relationships with other children.

4. Preliminary self-determination of the personality: relationships arise in the process of learning. Cognitive norms are being assimilated, and personal attitudes are being formed through differentiation among social relationships.

5. Economic relationships: a stage permitting the individual to validate his attitudes in a working environment and to establish his personal identity.

The model interprets social functioning in terms of information exchange. An optimal organization of the environment takes into account a relationship's specific character and minimizes information loss. The environment then can be measured objectively as a medium for transferring information.

1. Loss of information due to interference in the relationship.
2. Reduction in information loss when the conditions favor the relationship.

6. Relationships that give a person social value through activities freely initiated by him and through his participation in the cultural life of his time.

7. Relationships arising out of consumer activities.

8. Sexual relationships that serve to continue the generational process.

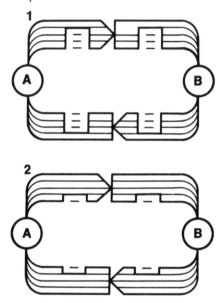

It is important to note that each stage can be defined in terms of its characteristic social relationships.

If we use historical analysis to give some concrete content to our analytical model, we can make the following observations that turn out to be useful and important:

1. In planning an environment we must conform to the dynamics of social relationships and their tendency to localize at specific centers of social organization.

2. We can substantiate the tendency of industrial and research complexes to isolate themselves and become relatively autonomous territorial structures, detached from the larger environment.

3. We must discover the influence of different social systems on urban life, that is, on the spatio-temporal organization of society in urban environments.

In classless primitive society, for example, we find a tribal village, its structure always reflecting the predominance in that society of relations based on kinship (houses for clan, separations marking other clans and brotherhoods). There is one unit of settlement: the tribal dwelling.

In the ancient era of slavery, the dominant role played by political relations, especially in the city, resulted in the physical dominance of structurally highly developed public buildings in urban centers (agora, forum, palace, temple). Three basic units of settlement were present: the city or **polis**, the manor as a productive unit, and the village.

With feudalism we see how the closed circle of relations governing each social class tended to isolate each class from the others; feudal lords lived in castle and court, peasant serfs in the village, and merchants and artisans in the town. There were still only three basic units of settlement.

With capitalism in the era of free competition, the dominance of economic relationships (i.e., the pursuit of immediate private profit and the intensive development of marketing) became the principal cause for the spontaneous, malignant growth of the industrial city. Happening at the expense of the village and the nonindustrial city, this led to the breaking up of villages into separate factory and farm communities. The fundamental units of settlement at that stage were the large expanding city, the small and stagnant town, the suburb, the village, and the farm.

In the era of monopoly capitalism a spontaneous dissolution of the large city takes place and intensifies the growth of suburbs. The fundamental components then become: the central city, the small satellite

Southern Cotton Plantation
in the Soviet Union

center (old and new) tending toward a certain optimum size, the workers' suburb, the factory town, the
village and farm, the industrial complex, the research
center, and the shopping center. Various institutions
and services move away from the city: hotels, movies,
stadiums, hospitals, schools, camps, etc. All these
elements are linked by a single transportation and

communication network. Together they constitute the megalopolis: the unplanned result of urban growth under contemporary capitalism.

Historical analysis thus reveals how the mode of production, being the sum of productive forces and relations of production, influences the spatial and temporal organization of the environment, not in a

23

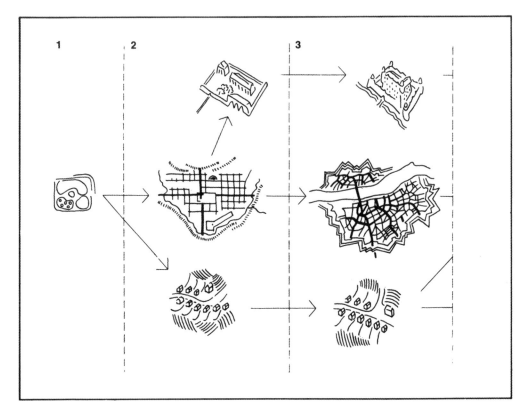

Change and discontinuity in the growth of social organization, with corresponding spatial and temporal effects on demographic patterns and urbanization.

1. Communal organization of primitive society: The structure of the environment corresponds to the predominance of a social system based on kinship. The community of tribal dwellings houses branches of a family and brotherhoods. There is one unit of settlement: the tribal village.

2. Slavery: The importance and intensity of political relationships are shown by the dominance of public building over all other forms in the ancient city: agora, forum, palace, and temple. There are three units of settlement: the **polis** or capital city, the agricultural holding, the village.

3. Feudalism: The closed circle of relationships within each class isolates classes from each other (the lords in their castles and rural holdings, the serfs in fields and villages, the merchants and artisans in towns).

4. Capitalism in the era of free competition: Buying and selling predominate over all other forms of association. The pursuit of private profit and the expansion of market relationships result in the predatory growth of the industrial city and in the dispersal of villages. At the same time farms are absorbed into large

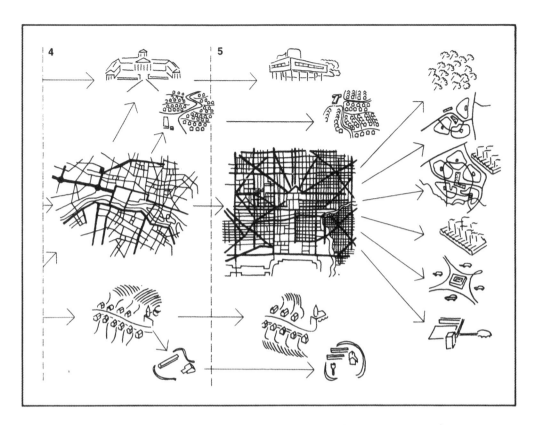

direct or mechanical way, but in an indirect one—through the specific kinds of relationship dominant in a given society.

In communism, also, the dominant kinds of human relationship will vitally influence the character of spatial and temporal organization.

The present situation shows that new communist forms of social relationship are developing within an inherited urban environment. Even the designs of buildings now being constructed rarely express the new structural criteria. This is understandable in a period of transition, since new functions, not yet having found their proper forms, are forced to assume old ones. Unlike similar transitional stages in the past, however, the present does not call on us

agricultural operations. The forms of social organization become: large cities in the process of unplanned expansion, small stagnating towns, residential suburbs, as well as factory towns, villages, and agricultural syndicates.

5. Monopoly capitalism: Spontaneous functional dissolution of the large city results in new agglomerations, including all the elements of its decaying core besides all the components of older forms of settlement.

simply to wait and see how the new communist environment will shape itself and then to note its characteristics. It is the special and historical claim of communism to be a work of conscious creation based on theory. We must begin to look at the prevalent forms of social relationships and to inquire into the effects they should produce historically on the whole spatio-temporal structure of communist life. This means that we should analyze the basic communist premises of society as elaborated by Marxist-Leninism and also the contemporary social realities that reflect these premises.

Such analysis leads to the basic conclusion that in classless communist society the predominant social relationship is creative and that in this society the individual has real and equal opportunities for the free and harmonious development of his own capabilities through creative work. The communist system, in fact, focuses on the individual and on his creative development.

Applied to an urban environment, this principle means that anyone living in a true communist society should enjoy equally with all others living anywhere in it conditions conducive to self-development and similar creative activity. Analysis of communist premises and our schematic model indicate both the basic social institutions and the phases of individual growth in communist society. This method also allows us to plan the lines of influence of society as a whole on the basis of each person's or each group's creative activities. Identification of the person or group with the social process defines what we mean by the functional structure (social matrix) of the urban environment and underlies its spatial and temporal organization.

Recognizing the intensive social interdependence that is required in a society built on automation in economic production and on collaboration in scien-

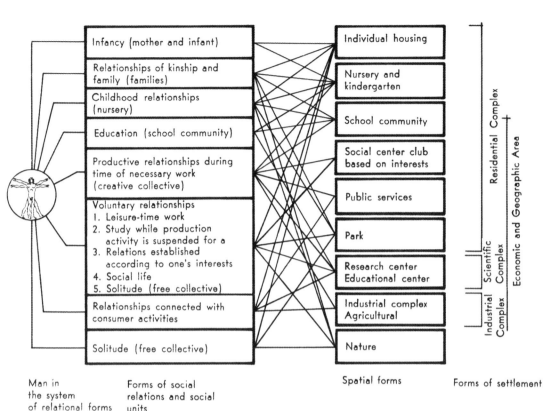

Man in the system of relational forms	Forms of social relations and social units	Spatial forms	Forms of settlement

Forms of social relations and social units:

- Infancy (mother and infant)
- Relationships of kinship and family (families)
- Childhood relationships (nursery)
- Education (school community)
- Productive relationships during time of necessary work (creative collective)
- Voluntary relationships
  1. Leisure-time work
  2. Study while production activity is suspended for a
  3. Relations established according to one's interests
  4. Social life
  5. Solitude (free collective)
- Relationships connected with consumer activities
- Solitude (free collective)

Spatial forms:

- Individual housing
- Nursery and kindergarten
- School community
- Social center club based on interests
- Public services
- Park
- Research center Educational center
- Industrial complex Agricultural
- Nature

Forms of settlement:

- Residential Complex
- Scientific Complex
- Industrial Complex
- Economic and Geographic Area

tific and creative work, we propose three systems of social interaction:

1. The research complex: a combination of laboratories, experimental projects in animal and plant cultivation, classrooms, libraries, and buildings for administrative personnel and central computers.

2. The residential complex: dwellings, nurseries, kindergartens, elementary and high schools, community parks with leisure facilities and areas, and other public services.

3. The industrial complex, which also includes organized agricultural production.

What we are proposing are patterns of settlement that are based on groups in the population. By so

The system of relationships in communism determines the functional structure of the environment.
Each type of construction is imagined as an element of the unified structure, which is presumed to be a general prototype.

27

doing we are taking note of the general tendency toward functional disintegration in modern cities. This tendency produces the isolation of industrial complexes and research centers into relatively autonomous units with a "daytime population" of commuters from the central city or suburbs. Obviously, these isolated units in their present form have neither acquired a distinctive character of their own nor have they become well-integrated systems within themselves. Because of their unplanned development, they function simply as elements accidentally juxtaposed with others in one vast urban agglomerate.

By contrast, each of our proposed examples is an integrated and systematic element that produces by means of functional social grouping a planned pattern of urban settlement. This concept of population grouping is appropriate to a society in which creative relationships dominate. For example, each of our proposed systems provides a frame of reference for people devoting a given amount of time (workday or week) to their occupation or to education befitting their age, family role, and personal interests.

To make this concept work, the subsystems making up the total urban environment must be well co-ordinated and in equilibrium with the whole. Working out their interrelationship in detail would require the collaboration of many specialists in many fields.

Unfortunately, we have only rather incomplete statistics so far and a few elementary indications of what may be the physical and psychological capacities of man, along with our still crude empirical expectations. Even on the basis of such incomplete data, however, we believe that we can draw some preliminary conclusions concerning the qualitative and quantitative characteristics of the communist urban environment and at least focus attention on this important question.

PRODUCTION AND THE URBAN

ENVIRONMENT

With electrification, automation, efficient production methods, and a reduced working day, production has come to consist of three fundamental sectors:

1. Automated industry
2. Scientific research and use of feedback from the machines themselves
3. Mass education—the formation of communist man

Each sector's capacity for absorbing manpower and territory creates a dynamic pattern of expansion with a corresponding effect upon spatial relationships within a given economic and geographic region.

Social relationships that are intrinsic to the production process nevertheless do not determine the character of future residential building.

Social relationships intrinsic to the production process are a formative and central factor in establishing each individual's personal identity. Only through productive interaction with others, using and testing his own abilities, and applying the knowledge acquired during his education does a person become a true member of society.

During the transition to communism, social relationships intrinsic to the production process undergo radical modifications as they respond to economic change and to all other relationships characteristic of classless communist society. The technical and scientific revolution now transforming large-scale production brings about striking changes in the human relationship to commodities, instruments of production, and the process of communication.

Electrification, automation, highly efficient production methods, and reduction of the working day are obvious aspects of this revolution. For example, electrification reduces the need for physical labor to the manipulation of controls. Since it can be generated and relayed almost anywhere to meet local power demands, electricity provides a centralized power system that favors the rational distribution of society's productive forces.[3]

Automation means that, wherever it seems possible and reasonable, the mental and physical work of man can be replaced by machine labor. This process ends old occupations, frees men from monotonous and uncreative work, and allows them to overcome the

The Scientific and Technological Revolution

[3] Cf., M. A. Vilanskij, **Electrification in the U.S.S.R. and the Distribution of the Productive Forces** (Moscow, 1963), pp. 175–203.

natural limitations of human physical and intellectual power. The direct connection between man and the objects and instruments of his work is being replaced by a new relationship: one between man and the automatic device. As his purely material involvement with the production process comes to an end, he takes up his position at the controls and handles the critical devices that regulate the flow of productive processes. Now the skill that is needed is the ability to evaluate quickly and correctly a situation described on an instrument panel that is linked to a production or research process.[4]

Automation involves both a substantial reduction of menial labor in material production and the upgrading of the qualifications of those who remain in that sphere of activity to the level of mechanical engineers. Automatic devices produce and regulate themselves, creating the most efficient means of doing their work. Man's role, then, is to program and control the labor of machines in a fully automated system of production.

Complexity of Production

Contemporary technical and scientific advances are realized in the material world through complex methods of production. Elements are separated and recombined; raw materials and partly processed material are put through a series of modifications. By-products are utilized, and waste is avoided. These are the chief characteristics of today's production procedures. The basic minimal unit of production, therefore, cannot be a single specialized factory or a simple combination of industries grouped together by happenstance, but rather a territorial organization of productive and industrial processes, in which complex yet rational functioning demands mutual

[4] Cf., A. I. Leont'ev, B. F. Lomov, **Man and Technology** ("Voprosy psichologij").

adjustments.[5] Within the industrial centers, and the economic and geographic regions defined by them, we find the most advantageous kind of specialization, co-operation, and placement of the units of production.

Automation opens up unlimited possibilities for machine specialization and for the consequent liberation of labor; indeed, for the liberation of the individual from the obligation to work at a single occupation all his productive life.[6] The resulting multiplicity and interdependency of human activities naturally create major problems of co-ordination. There must be co-operation among those who plan and direct parts of the productive process, as well as among those who engage in scientific research.

As the modern system of production grows, it demands men of various skills and in turn is influenced by their personalities. The wider the range of contacts of men who are performing specific jobs of co-ordination the higher will be their productivity and their ability to realize fully their own capabilities. The range

[5] Cf., N. N. Kolosovskij, **The Basis of Division into Economic Districts,** Moscow, 1958, pp. 39, 138, 143; V. V. Poksisevskij, **Crucial Problems of the Future Distribution of Production** ("Geograficeshie Problemy Krupnykh rajonov S.S.S.R."), Moscow, 1964, p. 19; A. E. Probt, **Distribution of Socialist Industry,** Moscow, 1962, p. 98.
[6] S. G. Strumilin, **On the Ways of Communist Construction,** Moscow, 1959, p. 12.

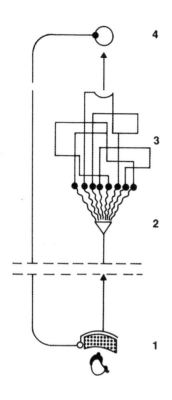

4

3

2

1

Man and the machine; a system. The man can be wholly isolated from every stage of mechanical production.
1. Control board
2. Regulatory system
3. Tools
4. Products

of their contacts includes both access to technical skill and association with administrative colleagues. Sometimes initiating contacts spontaneously, such a group of men tends to make the production system expand until it reaches the greatest possible output in both the central system and in all related subsystems (including subsidiary research centers) within a given economic and geographic district.

Those people who constitute the guiding productive force in the economy must be gifted with versatile personalities, "capable of orienting themselves anywhere in the whole productive system." [7] This means not only being able to move freely from one function to the next, or combining several functions, but working in teams when a complex problem requires a collective approach.

The working day can be reduced through the extraordinary growth in labor productivity, which in turn can be attributed to electrification, automation, and efficient production procedures. As this change takes place, the proportion of work time to free time changes radically. For the first time in the history of man, leisure time will exceed work time. The problem becomes "how to reduce to the minimum the time required for socially necessary work." [8] If we consider the demands that are apt to be made in various fields through the recombination of various kinds of labor, we can estimate that an individual's work time will tend to average approximately four hours per day.

From this summary of the changes produced by electrification, automation, and efficient production procedures (including the reduction of the work day), we can draw some conclusions of significance for our present study.

[7] K. Marx and F. Engels, op. cit., vol. IV, p. 33.
[8] Karl Marx, unedited manuscripts, **"Bolshevik"** (Moscow, 1939), 11–12, p. 62.

As communist production develops in space and time, three distinct levels of economic activity become apparent:

1. The level of automated production involves the entire productive process of extracting raw materials and reshaping them, producing the means and instruments of further production as well as articles of consumption. At this level the machine dominates. It produces a high level of material well-being. Human participation and intervention are minimal and consist almost entirely in running machines, checking equipment, and starting new manufacturing routines.

2. The educational level includes extensive institutions offering the instruction necessary to technical education. It sometimes means the use of special learning machines and generally requires the application of methods and devices resulting in a varied and well-co-ordinated training to meet all the needs of the fundamental areas of production. At this level the dominant element is man. As a student, he is the object of labor; as an instructor, he is its instrument; as a trained person graduated from a technical or professional course of study, he is also its product.

3. The scientific level of production uses a variety of means for receiving, storing, exchanging, and elaborating information concerning any field of human activity or nature. In this area the object, instrument and product of activity, whether performed by man or machine, is primarily information:

a) The initial data in the form of human or machine memory become the basic material.

b) Information that acts to transform other information, whether it be through operations of the human mind or through application of the algorithm or computer, can be considered an instrument of production.

c) New information, the result of initial information processed by human mental activity and by machine,

37

can be termed the product. Obviously, this third level of productive activity includes pure scientific research.

Collectivization of Science

In large-scale production today mental labor (scientific work and research) outweighs any other kind of human involvement. Science embraces all fields and all levels of production, and controls what is produced.

As a result of the mass production of information, and because of the complexity of the problems to be solved (which at times surpasses the cognitive powers of any individual), the character of mental labor has changed. Reception and communication of information and its modification at critical points are now not so much an individual as a collective process.

Nowadays any problem of a complex order impinges on several spheres of activity. Formulating and resolving a problem require a collection of people who can work together on its various aspects. Not only must each team member apply his specialty to the problem, but at the same time he must be generally knowledgeable. Above all, he must be able to collaborate with others on research and must be able to understand the whole problem and the technical language of his colleagues.

We are not concerned here with specialized research limited to a restricted circle of experts who sometimes speak an altogether separate language; rather, we are referring to the collective work of many individuals who, given a varied and well-co-ordinated training, can collaborate effectively to modify a set of initial data.

Nevertheless, we cannot expect the development of co-operative personalities or individual aptitudes and interests of the kind that enrich each person's preparation for a chosen field of work to happen automatically as the result of a new system of social

relationships. Rather, these are necessary precondi-
tions that must be fulfilled if every member of society
is to participate in valid creative work. Hence, questions of how to organize collective work—deciding
what should be the quantitative and qualitative composition of research teams—are of critical concern
and influence the principal area of human productive
activity today, namely, scientific inquiry, which is one
critical level of productive activity in general.

The technology of scientific work, including the
processes that modify data and store the vast
amounts of information flowing from meetings and

Dynamic in the spatial growth and in the growth of the capacity to absorb human beings in the three fundamental levels of productive activity.
1. Material production by means of machines
2. Formation of human beings
3. Science

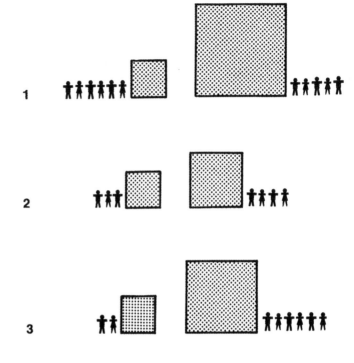

regular conferences, requires spatial definition (just as much as manufacturing processes and the interchange of raw and partly finished materials do).

Scientific institutions require the creation of centralized research centers. Such organizations in turn need a centralized system of communication to permit personnel from various institutes to gather with maximum speed at any given moment and, as a single collectivity, to exchange information from laboratories and related institutions. In such a scientific center there must be a single comprehensive system of information storage and exchange, besides a unified system of data storage and processing, so that each scientific team and each technician can receive whatever input he needs at any time and in any field of scientific knowledge.

Let us take the three sectors of productive activity and examine the broader relationships characteristic of each, their expansion rate in spatial terms, and their immediate capacity to absorb human labor.

Rapid territorial expansion in a given period of time is characteristic of machine production, first as its function of processing a supply of raw material grows and then as its subsidiary activities which tend to expand with the manufacturing enterprise itself, call for ever greater quantities of space.

The transportation of raw materials follows various routes that eventually join and make a functional set of interchanges among two, three, or four industrial complexes. These contacts may even generate an entire transportation system within a given economic and geographic region, as has actually happened in several of the most developed European industrial zones (Urals, Don Basin, Ruhr, Alsace-Lorraine, etc.).

Expanding production, with its accompanying demands for suitable space, is not something that a society should seek to limit inadvisedly, since such attempts would mean renouncing the satisfaction of its growing needs. The problem is not to limit growth as such, but to interrupt its linear continuity, to impose a systematic pattern and plan on its territorial expansion.

We have noted previously that the basic and most visible factors of economic growth are the industrial complex and its discontinuous expansion within an economic and geographic region. Planning therefore should envision the division of regions into industrial, agricultural, and residential zones. Accurate surveys of the natural resources within each region and plans for their use should help determine the division into zones. A dynamic plan for the communication and transportation systems should be worked out to join them together.

The industrial zones are divided into two types of spaces:
1. The world of the machines
2. The world of men
The world of the machines does not require careful spatial organization in respect to human needs. The uninterrupted automated production process works without the presence of men.
The world of men is found in research laboratories, in administrative offices, etc. Here we can find the basis for a direction for contemporary architecture.

Every industrial complex must be planned and built with an adequate allowance for the corresponding trends toward increased automation and decreased manufacturing time. These tendencies gradually differentiate two levels of production: that of the machine and man. Accordingly, a control center should be planned in the beginning to meet the needs of any well-co-ordinated and defined industrial complex. Various plant operations could then be unified by a single transportation system, which would mean, for one thing, that personnel could be carried to work at maximum speed.

The organization of agriculture presents a special problem. Assuming an abundant supply of electricity, any area if connected with centralized energy sources would have maximum potential power, light, and heat. In addition, artificial means of feeding and the use of stimulants for growth provide crops and livestock

with the best nutritive substances and accelerate their development. As a result, agriculture should be able to reduce its dependency upon local conditions (type of soil, atmospheric conditions and climate, even seasons, and the day-night cycle) as well as on the amount of available arable land. In the initial planning the areas of land to be cultivated should be laid out clearly with provisions for later reductions proportional to the global increase in production.

Ultimately, there must be a transformation of agriculture into a kind of industry based on the spatial unit of the rural and industrial zone that processes primary agricultural products by means of a common electrical and thermal energy system.

We confront another special problem of labor productivity in the service occupations. The spatial isolation characteristic of service activities (stores, warehouses, food distribution centers, eating places, domestic services) results from a preference for locating them within residential zones, even though this isolation puts a strain on the residential area's transportation system due to consignment, shipping, etc.

As for the service sector's capacity for absorbing manpower, we note two contradictory trends. On the one hand, there is an increase in both the quantity and variety of consumer goods, as well as in the number of centers where consumer transactions are carried on. While this tendency leads to an increase in employment, the very growth of services leads to mechanization; and self-service will prevail even if in the next ten years the capacity of this sector to absorb manpower still may increase considerably. As for spatial growth, we have already indicated (on the basis of a simple calculation) that a stabilization in the number of service facilities per capita will take place.

Machine-oriented economic activities clearly will undergo great territorial expansion as they generate industrial complexes, while agricultural zones will tend to stabilize. Employment in both presumably will decrease to a minimum.

On the other hand, the educational sector within this model of a communist society develops relatively stable patterns with regard to space utilization and number of persons employed. The facilities required are estimated on the basis of the number of persons of an age to receive instruction, the corresponding number of required teachers, and the amount of space normally allotted to an educational program.

As the scientific techniques and the actual scope of planning continue to develop, it seems that in spite of the wide use of teaching machines a significant growth will begin to take place in the educational sector's capacity to absorb manpower. This growth will come from increasing specialization of knowledge and from the complex activities involved in its application, particularly to functions like social planning.

Consequently, we can anticipate a spatial growth in
this area, a growth generated by the creation of new
scientific planning centers.

At this point, however, we expect the spatial expansion of the educational sector, even if growth is
continuous, to be far smaller, in absolute terms, than
the analogous spatial growth in the sector of mechanical production.

Research centers and planning institutes, together
with the educational institutions related to them,
constitute the basic element of spatial organization
in this sector. Again they are connected by a unified

Sketch of Functional
Relationships in a Zone
with Groups of
Urbanized Settlements

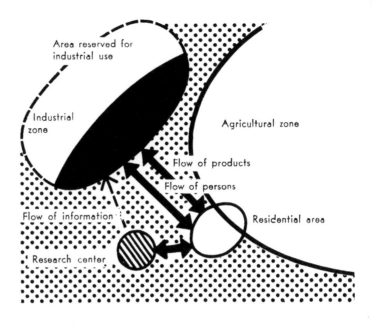

communication and transportation network linking
them to each other and to neighboring residential
and industrial zones.

**Proposals for
Spatial Distribution**

Comparing the basic functions of productive activity leads us to some conclusions about their spatial
distribution within economic and geographic regions
and the kind and amount of contact among sectors
within them.

The rapid extension of the industrial complex requires that ample open space be provided within a
given economic and geographic region. This reserved
space will constitute the larger part of the industrial
zone, and only industrial construction will be per-
mitted. However, the industrial zones can be contiguous with agricultural and residential ones, even if
areas of assimilation develop on either side of the
border between industrial and residential areas.

The tendency of agricultural areas to stabilize and
fuse at their border with industrial zones implies that
we should deliberately plan for industrial zones to be

Prefab Elements Used in
New Soviet Construction

47

surrounded by agricultural ones. Generally, residential zones are assumed to develop either as scattered settlements in agricultural areas or in conservation areas (parks and protected forest lands) that are not assigned to agriculture or industry.

The organization of centers for education and scientific planning represents a separate problem, since these are thought to be units that will increase at a constant though moderate rate. Since science usually is applied to production, one might think initially of locating the two functions near each other.

Spatial Correlation

The impact of science on production comes only after technological and mechanical developments, based on the programming of information, the making of models, and the elaboration of designs in the laboratory (in other words, on the kind of work undertaken in planning centers) have been accomplished. Scientific innovations in machinery and in production methods, moreover, are not often tested in actual industrial environments. When this is desirable, the test situation can be handled by organizing an information exchange and by shipping the material needed for a pilot project. Accordingly, these centers of scientific research need not be located very near industrial complexes.

Science does not study production alone, of course, but all nature and all society in their myriad interactions. Science is therefore at the same time both free from and dependent upon all areas of vital human activity. We should say then that scientific and educational planning centers represent an autonomous sector of productive activity. Since their specific location is determined by their intrinsic functions and the course of their development, we can foresee that in the immediate future the capacity of these centers to absorb manpower will increase enormously, while their spatial expansion will be moderate. Hence they will tend to be attracted to the residential zones where their workers live.

Designating locations for interconnected activities and organizing them in economic and geographic regions lead us to some ideas about plans for transportation and communication systems. The flow of circulation can be divided into three distinct streams:

1. A stream of commodities subdivided into, on the one hand, the flow of raw materials and partly manufactured components within the zone of production and, on the other (on completion of this cycle), the flow of finished products out of the zone.

2. A human stream (transportation to and from work), which can be divided into a main stream of labor pouring into the production area and branches distributing workers within it.

3. A stream of information, including all relationships and communication taking place between individuals, between machines, and between individual and machine.

If we assume co-operation among society's productive functions and allow for their potential capacities to absorb manpower and to expand in space, then we can determine the force of each sector and foresee how their communication systems will develop. Obviously, the major flow of material goods will take place within industrial complexes, between industrial complexes, and between industrial and residential zones. Human traffic will tend to be heaviest between residential zones and industrial complexes, and between residential zones and research centers. The plan anticipates the reduction of the work force in industrial complexes with a correspondingly heavier employment in the scientific centers. Within the centers themselves, traffic circulation becomes internal, like the flow of information itself, which is mostly contained within a research center or industrial complex.

Questions Concerning Social Relationships

From our analysis of social relationships, we can see what the principal forces are that shape the spatio-temporal development of a geographic and economic region, not only under present conditions but in the near future. This theoretical structure provides us with some guidelines and gives us a basis for planning applicable to any region.

Yet one cannot help observing how incomplete this proposed structure is. For example, one of the most important questions concerning contemporary urban environments remains unanswered: What residential arrangements should be provided for the workers in a production process organized according to the general schema given here?

Analysis of the production process cannot answer this question, for the housing of workers is a matter of absolute indifference from the point of view of production. Within a given economic and geographic zone, people can live in large, medium, or small cities, in workers' suburbs, in villages, or in groups of individual houses scattered through residential zones. From the point of view of production all that is necessary is that qualified workers be found at their posts in the mornings, well rested and full of energy, and that these men somehow raise their own capacities beyond what their work tasks impose on them. Except for these very abstract requirements, analysis of the production process does not tell us anything about the character or scale of desirable residential construction. This problem can be solved only by analysis of all the other forms of social interaction characteristic of classless communist society.

ORGANIZATION OF DAILY LIFE

In the present phase of social development the transformation of daily life waits upon the growth of public child care.

The residential complex will include low-rise buildings for overnight nurseries and elementary schools, and high-rise structures of standard residential units for adults. From both our analysis of the social implications of early child care and from our estimate of likely consumer service and transportation needs, two major substructures can be expected to appear in the new environment: the primary residential complex and the residential sector. Examination of the changed organization of daily life finally leads to predictions about the architectural characteristics of future housing.

For the contemporary architect the most interesting aspect of the complex urban environment is housing (from the simplest house to the most elaborate residential structure). Housing is pertinent to most of the objectives of current planning, decides the degree of their realization, and determines whether various different goals will prove compatible.

Questions about the organization of daily life are especially relevant today, since this area of ordinary routine now shows signs of rapid change.

Why expect a series of transformations in this aspect of life? Basically, because a clear and decisive improvement in the material well-being of the people can be expected to occur within the next two decades.

"Every family, including young couples, will have a hygienically adequate and comfortable home, a place suited to civilized living." [9]

"Conditions must make it possible to reduce and simplify the domestic labor of women. Public service should replace their labor and be able to satisfy the daily material needs of the family." [10]

"Extending the network of institutions for child care on a large scale will give every family the option of keeping their children in such institutions without charge through adolescence." [11]

Changes in the traditional family unit will directly affect all solutions to the housing problem. But such changes depend in many ways on the further devel-

Public Education

[9] **Program of the Communist Party of the U.S.S.R.** (Moscow, 1961), p. 94.
[10] Ibid., p. 97.
[11] Ibid., p. 98.

opment of public education, concerning which there is a good deal of controversy among parents and educators.

Those who believe in raising children at home see two justifications for public child-care institutions. First, the fact that parents are too busy, and second, the need to isolate children from bad parents. Generally, however, as the amount of free time increases and educational standards rise, the need for a system of public education covering the child's complete life will diminish, and every couple possessing material comforts and necessities can be expected to raise their own children to maturity.

On the other hand, in the present formative stage of communism, society is seriously concerned with child rearing and with the competence required of those involved. This task requires educators with a great deal of biological, psychological, medical, esthetic, and other sorts of training. It demands that responsible persons be able to apply such disciplines to specific situations and that they be experienced in doing so. It also demands that they show a specific disposition and love for teaching children of a particular age. These qualifications mean that those engaged in raising the next generation must truly have a pedagogical vocation and be scientifically trained. Mere experience of life and paternal or maternal sentiments are not enough to equip a person to teach correctly a member of society.

It is also said that a socialized system of education is inhumane toward parents, for it takes their children away and does not give them a chance to see them and participate in their education. This error is based on present practice, which locates most child-care centers and schools far from the homes of parents. This has happened partly because of the need to remove children from the poor hygienic conditions of overcrowded neighborhoods and partly because of the principle of assigning places in schools on the basis of the parents' place of work. Once we have good new housing, however, it will be possible to locate all child-care institutions in the immediate residential neighborhood.

The proper development of full-time public education will require large staffs. Many parents (besides those choosing the profession of teacher) can give their free time to kindergartens and public schools, where their own offspring are being educated.

The arguments of those who defend public child rearing are stronger, in our opinion, than those of the opposition. Their ideas, however, sound rather hypothetical as yet, because they lack positive evidence and cannot offer a clear and precise model to contrast with the traditional system. Developing such a model requires an objective study of the forms of social interaction, especially at the early stages of personality formation.

Contact with their peers is certainly valuable to children. In early childhood these contacts come through group play, an important activity from the fourth or fifth year of a child's life to the eighth or tenth. Play itself, in modern educational thought, is a fundamental method of preschool and school instruction. The success of a child's work in the first and second grades in reading and writing and arithmetic depends to an extent on the games of the earlier years.

The best opportunity for contact among children of preschool age occurs in the nursery, which is the best setting for developing the child's imitative powers and individual activities. He expresses his inclinations most freely here, and his egocentricity is least harmfully repressed.

The positive value of group activity, of course, is fully realized only when it is organized and directed

Childhood and Education

by educators who have benefited from advanced social training.

The largest desirable size of a group of children must be experimentally determined. The findings of experimental psychology indicate that an individual adult is capable of giving his attention to and controlling simultaneously up to fifty-seven objects. Therefore, with such complex objects as children to supervise, an educator probably should be assigned no more than six children at once.

During his play periods, a child should have the opportunity to relate to others of preschool age, either younger or older, so that in a wide range of games and roles he has a chance to develop his various natural abilities. Mixing a primary group of preschool children with another older or younger age group creates a double cell: two age groups and two teachers. The primary group (six children and one

teacher) and the double cell (twelve children and two teachers) may be used as our module in working out the structure of a child-care center.

The organization of double cells and the series of groups required for a child-care center covering the whole elementary cycle from the preschool grades through the school grades gives us the following minimum capacity for any one institution: six age combination groups (each containing one primary group from each grade of the four included in elementary school).

To this should be added the structure of the nurseries whose fundamental functions are:

1. To provide mothers with help and advice in the initial period of child rearing.

2. To prepare children three and four years of age for kindergarten and to develop their capacity for imitation and learning through collective play.

If we make a numerical estimate of these transitional groups, the basic number needed for the functioning "nursery-elementary school" is not less than about 216 pupils (or a multiple thereof). Such a capacity calls for a staff large enough to make possible a full range of specialists in every sector of preschool education (incluhing moral and esthetic education, medical supervision, music, drawing, dancing, arithmetic, construction).

What the Modern School Is Attempting to Do

Through play and relationships with adults, the informational system of the child, itself a particular kind of relationship, is gradually fed and reinforced, and learning takes place. By the eighth or ninth year of life, formal learning experiences begin to shape the child's social experience. He moves into a new stage of development and slowly becomes aware of himself as a human being with an autonomous personality.

The fundamental purpose of any school providing general education is to forge within the group and by means of the group a well-rounded and harmoniously developed human being, "a new individual who harmoniously combines in himself spiritual riches, moral purity, and physical perfection." [12] The school should help its pupil to find his own vocation and develop it, not by restricting him but by opening up to him all the fundamental fields of human knowledge. He can then creatively relate all sorts of knowledge to the pursuit of his own interests and to his relationships with his peers.

Eccentric development and professional deformation can be avoided only if pupils who represent diverse vocational tendencies continue to develop within the framework of a single institution. The students' inevitable specialization and eventual choice of vocation are possible within large general school

[12] **Program of the Communist Party of the U.S.S.R.,** op. cit., pp. 120, 121.

communities, well equipped and able to attract a well-qualified staff of teachers. These are preferable to various separate vocational schools, for only these large educational complexes can guarantee teaching specialized enough in all the fundamental areas of human activity to produce both a well-rounded and culturally aware person, and one who has developed a specific skill.

If we accept the conventional division of teaching into eight disciplines (sociology, education, the liberal and fine arts, biology, chemistry, mathematics, and engineering), specialization in one of these fields can develop in the course of an eight-year program as follows:

Class I–IV. Common curriculum for all students, with a supplementary program for those who are artistically talented and seminars for those who show promise in mathematics and physics.

Class V–VI. Specialization in two general directions: the humanities and the sciences.

Class VII. Further specialization along four distinct lines: socioeconomic; artistic and literary; chemical and biological; physical and mathematical.

Class VIII. Final specialization in one of the eight fundamental categories indicated above.

Practical experience in today's schools, as well as the findings of psychology, suggests that no more than twelve pupils should be assigned to each group in elementary school. This number should be maintained in the specialized courses of the upper level classes, although it can be doubled to twenty-four pupils in general courses.

Since each field includes about six to ten special subdivisions, the creation of primary groups within subdivisions will encourage co-operation among students who are entering a course of professional specialization. The number of graduates in any special field should also be a sign whether satisfactory working relationships developed with schoolmates in more advanced classes.

If we assume that the minimum number for a group specializing in an advanced field is six persons, the number graduating with a vocational training will range between thirty-six and sixty. Taking a statistical average, we shall assume forty-eight students, or four groups of twelve.

The sum of graduates in the eight areas of professional specialization will be 384.

If we now compute the functional structure of the school community as described above, we arrive at a total of 3,072 students. This gives us an approximate basis for estimating its size and for planning its buildings.

To complete his education, that is, to receive the right and the opportunity to work in a particular branch of social production, the graduate of a school of general education must take a supplementary course in his special field. This course can take from several months to several years, depending upon the student's specialty. In principle, however, this training is distinct from general education and constitutes a second stage in his professional development. It is completed at large educational centers such as universities or technical and professional schools that have been assimilated by general institutes of technology.

Throughout the whole cycle of public education the child's relationship with his family complements and guides his relationship with his peers in school.

While the child is in preschool, his contact with his parents will be fairly intensive. The parents will actively participate in his education and spend considerable time in the institution itself. For this reason, the institution should be close to the parents' residence.

During the time of the child's education in the gen-

eral school community, the relationship with his parents changes in character. Contact becomes less frequent (only a few times a week) and is related to holidays. Hence the interaction of children and their parents may take place either within the educational institution or in the parents' home. In either case, it requires a specific and yet to be defined spatial organization.

To sum up:

1. The first foundations of communist personality are established in nurseries through the relationship of children with their peers in preschool groups. The personality further develops in primary groups during the earliest grades. These are excellently suited to foster the unfolding of all aspects of a child's potential.

2. The personality formation that is richly developed in a number of directions must also take place through a shared educational process. This requires a careful subdivision of experience into two stages: general education (in a school community) and professional education (at a higher academic institution).

3. Nurseries and elementary-grade schools, school communities for general education, and advanced institutions will constitute separate building complexes.

Efficient communication must link the school with the child's home. Therefore, schools for younger children ought to be within a radius of 100 yards to 150 yards of home; the secondary school community should be within walking distance (a radius of one-half to three-quarters of a mile); higher academic institutions should be linked to the home by twenty minutes to thirty minutes of public transportation.

Types of Residential Structure

With the development of full-time public education, the traditional functions of family housing will be taken over by three new types of residence:

1. The residential units attached to the preschool and elementary school.

2. Residential quarters attached to the secondary-school community.

3. Apartment-type units for individual adults or for couples who are parents.

This list can be made more complete by adding certain more specialized kinds of housing, such as dormitories at higher academic institutions, homes for older persons requiring personal care, and hotel-type accommodations in resort areas meeting the vacation schedule of workers.

Let us, however, consider only the three fundamental types.

The basic housing unit attached to the nursery and elementary school will be a complex of two dormitories for twelve children (six in each), two rooms for play, two bathrooms, a room for teachers, and auxiliary space. The whole will not exceed an area of 2,000 square feet.

Housing for the general population will be substantially altered, yet its fundamental purpose will remain the same. The human being needs a private place where he can separate himself from others, rest, sleep, and live his family life. Housing must respond to these needs; it must create conditions suited to restoring the physical and moral forces that a man expends in his productive and social life.

These demands will continue to exist in the immediate future; in fact, they may become rather more pressing.

The more intense the social interaction and the wider a person's relationships the more he must be able to regenerate the energies socially expended, and the more profound and complete must be his physical and mental relaxation.

How much space does an individual need for this?

What should be the standard type of housing that not only can guarantee functional necessities, but also can provide the best conditions for psychological privacy?

As experience shows, existing housing, when judged by these standards, is far from ideal. The tendency to increase the amount of space allocated to individual housing is clearly understandable under the circumstances. It can decrease, however, as the more rational planning of housing units separates private from public functions and services. Then it would seem reasonable to use a residential standard of not more than 225 square feet per person (on the average).

This assumes a small number of persons living permanently in each apartment and the development of public eating places within residential buildings. The preparation of food in the family unit will no longer be necessary, but merely optional. The stove and kitchen cease to be the focal points of a residential plan. Minimal kitchen facilities can be included in a living room or foyer, and the space thus freed can be used for other needs, such as more spacious bathrooms.

The basic plan for an apartment divides it into two sections: rooms for daytime use and others for nighttime use. Furthermore, for the privacy of a married couple, it is essential to be able to subdivide the space into two ample areas for husband and wife.

The apartment should also provide a separate room for children during the hours and days that they visit their parents. Approximately fifty square feet to seventy-five square feet should be allocated for each child's play, sleep, and other activities.

Both expanded public services and areas in the residential building and reduction in the number of permanent inhabitants per apartment permit us to think in new ways about planning the interior. Instead of a series of little rooms lined up along a wall we imagine a single open space that runs the whole depth of the building and ends in windows on two opposite sides.

Bilateral orientation becomes more than a means for assuring greater freedom in planning the interior

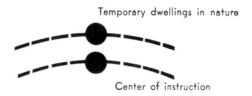

Temporary dwellings in nature

Center of instruction

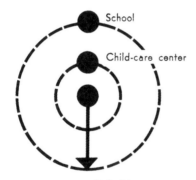

School

Child-care center

Pedestrian access

or an important principle of cross-ventilation for healthy living. Bilateral orientation signifies a new principle in the construction of housing and could mean the end of psychological restrictions and discomfort.

The principle of bilateral orientation is especially important in cases where apartments are located above the ground; in other words, where direct access to nature is replaced by visual contact. Here there is no substitute for a variety of views from windows.

Architects at present do not concern themselves much with "views." Yet it is precisely the view that has a most powerful influence upon the individual's psychological state when he is living in the limited space of an apartment. The view works as an extension of interior space and becomes an integral part of the world in which the individual is living. The visual relationship binding a person to his surroundings cannot be replaced by any degree of comfort in the internal arrangement of the home. This is why, no matter what technical solution the future residential architect may provide, bilateral orientation will retain its importance as a basic principle of planning. Any proposals for future housing that ignore this principle are unlikely to be successful, from the visual point of view, even though they might be satisfactory in every other respect.

The way in which apartments are combined determines the character of a building. Two aspects of the problem always seem to be in conflict. On the one hand, there is the desire for comfort in the apartment and for a link with green outdoor spaces; on the other hand, there is the need for economy in using available open space.

Ideal conditions for rest and privacy are offered by the individual house situated in the midst of nature. But this is an expensive kind of well-being. To give one family the comforts of life in the heart of nature, the costs of construction must be paid, as well as the cost of a series of individual services, from the refrigerator to the laundress to the automobile. The villa is the traditional retreat of the leisured minority at the top of the bourgeois society. The attempt to make the villa available to the average consumer means building a mass of little houses, each on a tiny piece of land. This method entails a minimum of domestic services, fairly satisfactory shared services, and transportation to meet individual needs.

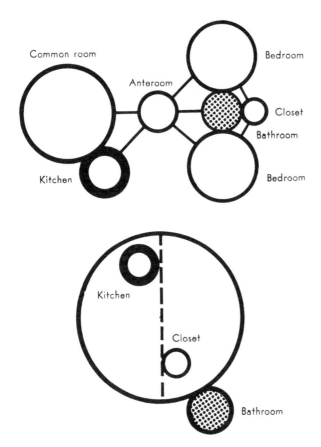

Common room

Anteroom

Bedroom

Closet

Bathroom

Kitchen

Bedroom

Kitchen

Closet

Bathroom

Functional plans of the traditional and the future residence. Instead of small isolated rooms, a single large space.

The mass construction of individual houses, however, destroys the basic character of this type of residence. There is no longer the possibility of isolation in nature. What results is a chaotic and depressing agglomeration of dwellings covering enormous stretches of land. This is obvious, for example, in the case of some new American cities and suburbs. At the same time, given the conditions of social equality and the increasing growth of demand for housing in our country, the search for a future kind of residential building leads logically to high-rise structures.

The spatial isolation of apartments in high-rise residential blocks allows the concentration of a very large

69

Monotonous stretches of individual low-rise houses

number of people in a relatively small space and the creation of an efficient system of services. Moreover, even with high density, considerable green spaces can be provided for the development of gardens and parks.

Bilateral orientation of apartments combined with the high-rise-building concept assures great privacy for each unit and large sweeping views. Proper site planning of high-rise buildings among green areas can make it possible to place low-rise children's institutions as near as possible to home. The real advantages of low-rise structures can then be enjoyed by our society, but according to different precepts from those of bourgeois society, that is, not by whoever can pay the most but by those who need these structures most, especially young children.

Our construction industry will soon be able to mass-produce reinforced-concrete structural components and lightweight infill panels. This means that in large projects standard residential construction can change from a brick-bearing wall system with five floors per building to prefabricated concrete units that allow

a more flexible subdivision of interior space and a greater number of floors. We can expect fifteen-story to seventeen-story residential structures to become common.

Present housing practice requires society to provide a great variety of apartments to meet the needs of families with different numbers of permanent resident members. As we move to full-time public education, however, the number of different apartment types can be reduced to a few, since their size will be determined only by the number of adults in the family. For children's visits, a single room will suffice, although its area can be increased for a number of children by reducing the size of other rooms in the apartment.

In conclusion, we suggest only three basic residential prototypes: one for the single individual (with or without children); one for the couple (with or without children); and one for two couples (a generation of older people, a younger couple, and children). This last type represents, in substance, a combination of two units of the second type, including a double allot-

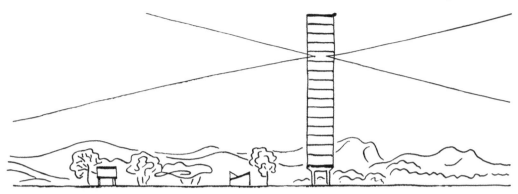

Different types of housing: (1) residence of one floor for small children, with direct access to garden; (2) residence of two floors for students—windows on garden; (3) residence of many floors for adults. Bilateral orientation of apartments—wide horizons visible from windows.

ment of bathroom and kitchen facilities.

Under these conditions there is no need to distinguish between buildings of different apartment types. Instead, we note a trend toward standard residential structures, each containing prototype apartments

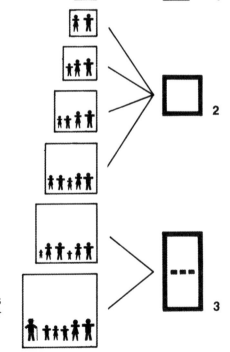

As public education develops, the number of types of apartment will be decisively reduced: (1) apartment for single individual; (2) apartment for one generation of adults and children; (3) apartment for two generations of adults and children.

and conforming to a standard construction system and layout of facilities. With such a universal system any variation on the family nucleus can be foreseen and provided for.

In considering the basic apartments or residential units, we have come to realize that the solution of the housing problem brings about important changes that are not merely mechanical but signify a general improvement in the quality of residential life.

The normal spatial area required for a child's upbringing, for example, will be distributed among three types of housing: the respective dormitories of elementary and secondary schools, and the family apartment. On the whole, the adult will need a proportionately larger area for living space than the child. This is wholly justified, as long as the child spends a considerable amount of time playing in the fresh air, or meeting in classes and assembly halls, while the adult, during the hours he is alone, has an acute need for individual space.

Different types of residence are not related in the same way to nature. For example, preschool-age pupils need a daily and direct relationship with nature, while older students can make frequent journeys into the open country and so gain direct contact with the earth and larger-scale natural environment. Hence, though the very young are better off in ground-floor housing, older children can live in multistory buildings.

Finally, for the more mobile group—that majority of adults who spend a relatively small part of the day at home—we should accept the high-rise residential structure. The loss of immediate contact with the outdoors at ground level and the need for daily use of an elevator are compensated in this situation by a bilateral orientation of views and, above all, weekend visits to temporary hotel-type residences, where relationships with nature are restored.

Variety in residential units results in a unified system that rationally allocates space according to function.

The residential system includes: kindergartens, individual houses, school communities, and apartment blocks. These are the basic elements of residential construction. Through their interrelationships they determine the size and shape of subdivisions in the new residential area. The functional relationships among them, which we have delineated by analyzing patterns of communal living, are precisely what brings us now to other aspects of the housing question, such as public transportation and communal services.

**Planning
Residential Areas**

The daily contact of preschool children with their parents requires, as we observed earlier, that residential buildings be in the immediate neighborhood of the children's school. In fact, the whole communal complex, even the detailed layout of prototype residential units, is organized on the basis of relationships between members of each group.

In principle, the planning of a primary residential complex permits all kinds of solutions: a system of low-rise buildings, a group of prefabricated units of varying heights, or a single high-rise building. In every case, however, the residential complex is not simply a conglomeration of dwellings but a social and spatial community. The apartment loses the autonomy of the single-family house. It is a unit that is unthinkable apart from the existence of the whole, and it therefore becomes the primary element in a collective system of housing.

To determine the size of population in the primary residential community, we can take the approximate number that we have established for each preschool institution (216 pupils) and the percentage of the population consisting of children from three to nine years old presently enrolled in the preschool and elementary system (thirteen per cent to fourteen per cent of the general population). This method leads us to a total of from 1,600 to 1,700 individuals (approximately 1,000 adults) per residential complex. When we consider the accompanying public services and consumer activities, we discover again the rationality of proposing a primary residential community of this size. To arrive at estimates of capacity, that is, to establish the number of persons that a center for consumer activities can easily serve, we must determine what kinds of service are to be provided and then estimate the potential demand for them, keeping in mind what the maximum distances between home and consumer service should be.

Two fundamental kinds of services should be distinguished among consumer needs. In the first category are the kinds of service that should efficiently provide the population with articles of daily use. These services should offer an assortment of goods and should be within a short walking distance of home. The second category of service includes the movie theater, pharmacy, swimming pool, ball park, local administration offices, café, restaurant, etc.

The practice in urban planning has been to distinguish very clearly between these two categories of commerce. In traditional English cities the microsector provides primary services at a distance of no more than 400 yards from a residential complex. Commerce has a fairly low density, and major traffic does not enter this microsector. Aside from the primary residential complex, there is a school for approximately every 6,000 persons. Services of the secondary category, on the other hand, are found in a town or neighborhood center with a population of over 20,000 persons. Usually these services are at highway intersections, and the shopping area is limited to about half a mile in any direction.

In mentioning foreign experience in the planning

of microsectors, we must remember that our own present residential system is based on four- or five-story units and thus considerably exceeds the density of the English neighborhood. Because of prevailing standards in Soviet housing, moreover, we need a more complete and more accessible system of public services than is required in foreign countries, where housing can be counted on to include adequate kitchen facilities for individual housekeeping.

This accounts for the considerably different features of our existing microsectors. Within a radius of about 400 yards to public transportation (seven minutes' walk) we concentrate 10,000 to 12,000 persons. Furthermore, each of our microsectors contains not one but two schools, occupying a relatively large amount of space and lying within range of public transportation. The primary services within the residential center generally seem to be insufficient for this population density and seem especially to be too far away from people's homes.

The desire to correct these faults has led city planners to formulate a whole new group of ideas centered on linking services and housing as closely as possible. These plans provide primary complexes of public services for every 1,000 to 4,000 persons within an effective radius of 300 feet to 500 feet. The result could favor a more intensive community life, because a fairly small group of residents, in face-to-face contact with workers providing the services, could correct and regulate the consumer activity in accordance with felt needs. Supplementary services, such as public-assembly halls, studios, special transportation needs, could also be arranged easily.

Approximate figures based on present service needs in large apartment houses and in microsectors indicate that a population of about 1,000 adults per primary unit would work very well.

In the present phase of development there are at

least two possible ways to organize these services.

The first option is to provide services at three levels: a primary level located within the residential complex; a nucleus of secondary services (food stores, clubs, etc.) within the microsector; a third nucleus of services (cinema, club, park, sports center, etc.) planned in the center of the larger sector. The system resulting from this organization of services is awk-

77

A new functional
residential structure will
replace the microsector.
1. Plan of the microsector
   traditional in England
2. Plan of the microsector
   characteristic of Soviet
   building practice
3. System of three levels
   of consumer services
4. Two levels of consumer
   services: pedestrian
   walkways are crossed by
   highways
5. Proposal: two levels of
   services. Rapid transport
   segregated from
   pedestrian traffic; school
   at periphery of built-up
   residential area

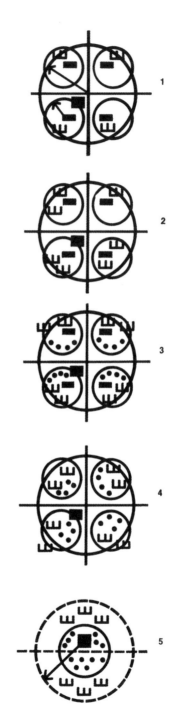

ward, however, and has few advantages, because the services are distributed too thinly among three kinds of consumer centers. This organization also leads inevitably to useless duplication.

The second possibility is to combine the two primary levels of service and locate the new single unit in one or several residential buildings. This leaves the third in the center of the larger sector, probably at a crossroads. Here an important disadvantage arises. Since it is not practical to locate all needed services in the residential complexes, we make the residents dependent upon the center of the sector. Since these primary-service levels cannot include a large food store (still less can they compete with large stores in selling manufactured goods) the system demands that residents cross large streets when they go to the shopping center.

Clearly, the analysis of service distribution in residential sectors leads to an attempt to separate vehicular from pedestrian traffic. This would enable us to plan the whole sector in a unified way and to enlarge its major shopping center, while primary services remain immediately accessible.

Solutions to the problem of urban transportation always depend upon interrelationships, which in turn are shaped by the preceding development of residential areas. We can be sure, at least, that the new kind of residential sector, constructed with commuter in mind, will be supplied with some form of rapid transit. This system should be planned from the beginning to avoid conflicts of cross-circulation for pedestrians, both for their safety and for the efficiency of the transportation system.

It is hardly necessary to add that private individual transportation has produced such an overwhelming set of unresolved problems in cities that even planners in bourgeois societies are inclined to limit it. In modern practice, planning has come to include subways running underground at a moderate depth, as well as elevated electric trains. The economic advantages of such a transportation system for getting commuters to and from production areas are obvious, and it is also an answer to congestion in the central city.

Having established that public transportation is to be separated from pedestrian circulation, we propose that large-scale residential structures in each sector be planned around a central pedestrian space. In this space will be a subway or elevated station, as well as consumer service centers and some light industry, if desirable. Pedestrian access accordingly determines the size of the residential sector. The larger the population that is to be housed in the sector the more easily we can justify localizing all needed services.

High-rise residential construction (even with children's institutions of only one to three floors) permits fairly high density of settlement, and it gains the advantage of efficient land use for this plan for an urbanized sector.

If we place the secondary-school community at the periphery of the residential sector (just within reach of pedestrian access), we gain interior density.

Assuming a maximum walking distance from home to the area of services and public transportation of about 500 yards, and a maximum straight-line distance of 100 yards from secondary school to home, the density we established earlier allows us to plan for 25,000 to 35,000 persons per sector. This number corresponds to our estimated capacity for the secondary-school community. In fact, it correlates with the fact that a school complex of 4,000 students corresponds to a population of 20,000 to 35,000 inhabitants.

The future residential sector will include the following distinct elements:

1. A system of services organized on two levels: the primary level of services as near as possible to home,

and the other located in a much larger and centralized shopping and commuting center.

2. Children's institutions for preschool and elementary education to be located as near as possible

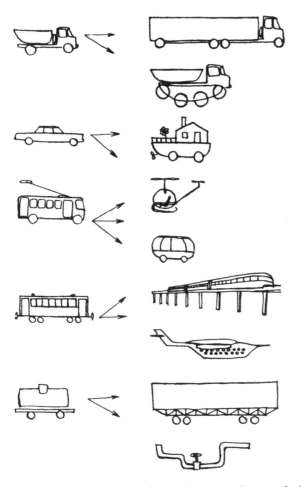

Evolution of Means of Transportation

to home; secondary schools at the periphery of the residential sector.

3. A public-transportation terminal within the shopping center, but not interfering with pedestrian circulation.

Two basic subdivisions become the obvious means

81

of organizing a total residential area. They are: (1) the residential complex of 1,500 to 2,000 persons; (2) the residential sector of 25,000 to 35,000 persons.

We have used visible present trends to plan our residential communities. Our conclusions are based on the consideration of coming conditions that can be reasonably foreseen.

It is not difficult to imagine that in time a new attitude will develop toward density and that new means of transportation and a more effective organization of collective services will suggest residential patterns characterized by altogether different criteria. It is sufficient to mention the possibility of gathering an entire residential area in a single macrostructure.

To sum up, we have here considered the basic problems that must be solved in reorganizing daily life, and we have analyzed the forms of communal life opened up by the technical and economic possibilities of the immediate future. Although our thinking has included the definition of residential units, we have not defined the architectural character of the new environment.

We know, however, that full-time public education for children, progressive extension of public services and transportation, and a high density in construction can all be realized in practical terms, given any size of residential population area.

LEISURE TIME

The twentieth century confronts mankind with the problem of leisure time, that is, with the problem of freedom. Freely developed social interactions are vital to vigorous urban life. Computations based on probability suggest that a fully developed cultural life can emerge and that a recognizable urban nucleus can form on a social base of at least 100,000 population. This is the new element in urban environments; this is the sociospatial unit of the new society.

Life structured by freely chosen relationships represents the fullest, most well-rounded aspects of each human personality. These are developed through choices made during the time free from work, on the basis of interests, desires, and cultural options open to all.

Freely Chosen Relationships as a Function of Leisure

The twentieth century is the first to pose seriously the question of how to make use of the leisure time available to the laboring masses, who have just begun their self-liberation from the full-time working day.

In the coming years, with the reduction of the work day to five or six hours and the parallel reduction of other chores, leisure time will consist of about six to seven hours per day.[13] If we further decrease the work day to a period of not less than four hours and assume a minimum system of daily services, leisure in the next decade may increase to an average of eight to nine hours per day, not counting holidays or the extended annual vacation.

The increase in leisure time in coming years will present a social problem of extraordinary significance: how to make use of this free time in a manner consistent with the communist ideal, that is, how to use it in the interests of each and all.

To resolve this problem it is necessary to examine leisure activity as a process distinct in character yet part of the general process of community life. Leisure activity creates numerous individual and material needs. These mean that areas must be assigned to leisure activity, areas that, of course, should be fully accessible to everyone.

From this point of view we can structure the kinds

[13] S. G. Strumilin, **Our World in Twenty Years** (Moscow, 1964), p. 91.

of leisure activity characteristic of the period of transition to communism as follows:

1. Activities that promote fellowship and broaden professional interests.

2. Activities that train one either to become more qualified in one's own field or to qualify for a different sphere of work.

Considering the sudden increase in the number of people studying while holding full-time jobs and considering that this increase is attributable to the shortening of the workday in 1959 by one hour, we can predict with confidence that successive additions to free time will produce a situation where a large majority of the population will engage in some form of study. Friendship, too, can be viewed as a form of free relationship and can be related to work and study, since it involves meditating on and evaluating in communication whatever problems and interests arise for an individual in his development.

We have already considered the desirability of planning for residential privacy. Free relationships can easily develop anywhere that privacy is provided in the context of community life, whether the place be attached to a residential unit, an educational center, a research center, or a place of work. Any of these can foster associations based on interest and desire. The purpose of free relationships is to encourage an individual to develop his capacities in full, to attain insight, and to grow in accord with that insight. Free association with other persons has been less studied than other forms of human relationship. Nevertheless, the development of this kind of association also requires suitable spatial planning.

Associations based on shared interests combine a number of functions. They range from useful and cultural recreation, which widen a person's horizons and elevate his intellectual level, to activities that lead to a new profession. This kind of association is becoming common enough to make it a consideration in all urban planning from now on.

In our country the club, gallery, museum, library, and theater are focal points that bring people together for cultural activities. The university and the popular theater also foster these interests .

Unfortunately, inadequacies in the planning and correlation of leisure activity are obvious everywhere. Smaller cities have a network of cultural institutions, but their potential is usually mediocre. The cultural offerings of neighboring small cities are rarely co-ordinated or raised to certain standards, as they ought to be. Consequently, considerable leisure time is being wasted. In many ways the individual's self-development is poorly supported by society, since all possible channels of information are by no means used to their real potential to communicate cultural and general events, to disseminate scientific and technical discoveries, etc. Yet such stimulation renews the individual by arousing his natural desire for more knowledge, by suggesting new goals in his field of work, and by helping him to direct his energies toward the common good.

The wasteful overconcentration of cultural values in very large cities leads to huge agglomerations of millions of persons there; yet even the capital city is incapable on a national scale of satisfying the desire of the masses for scientific knowledge, or the individual's desire for self-development. It is this discrepancy that has strengthened voluntary associations and given rise to leisure activities based on common cultural interests. This type of social organization must overcome the contradictions in the cultural life of both city and small town.

"Eventually, with the realization of another formidable rise in the material level of culture there will be established . . . an expanded network of libraries, reading rooms, theaters, cultural centers, clubs, cinemas . . . a vast development of popular universities, repertory theater companies, and other cultural organizations . . . a great chain of film and art studios connected with technical and scientific laboratories, so that all those who show creativity and interest in this particular direction can participate in this kind of work.

"As a matter of policy, we must uniformly distribute across our national territory cultural institutions that are designed to raise the cultural life of small towns to the level of the great cities and also to sponsor a rapid cultural development in newly reclaimed areas." [14]

The Club for Cultural and Scientific Projects

The individual's broad human development and social fulfillment through cultural activities are considered extremely important today and are being realized through free association. To meet such aspirations we must plan the new urban environment to include a large proportion of people representing each fundamental field of human knowledge and to provide such people with ways of forming groups devoted to their cultural interests.

Considering that the successful pursuit of cultural concerns always requires a certain amount of equipment, books, instruments, etc., a cultural association would be organized: (1) to meet a required standard on a par with the current work in that field; (2) to include enough qualified persons to maintain a lively level of activity in the field. Each club should have a nucleus of enthusiastic enrolled members who regularly devote part of their leisure time to the association.

In our opinion, the club is the best form of organization for a voluntary group pursuing specific cultural interests, for it permits the most varied communica-

[14] **Program of the Communist Party of the U.S.S.R.** (Moscow, 1960), pp. 130–131.

tion in the free pursuit of learning. There can be systematic courses or occasional lectures; seminars on chosen topics; conferences, debates, discussions, and public or private conversations. Individual and group initiative are equally applicable. There can be informative exhibits showing the results of any particular inquiry or reflecting the activities of members. Presentations can be made on any aspect of art (film, theater, concerts, etc.). Without limiting the individual's freedom, this form of flexible association can satisfy any level of interest in a field.

Depending upon public interest, knowledge gained through these associations can become generally available through lectures and discussions, reports, seminars, debates, and art exhibits. All these activities give people the opportunity to obtain a great deal of information in various fields, to explore current problems, as well as acquire or use a variety of books, reproductions, films, records, etc.

A higher and relatively more time-consuming level of cultural participation would involve regular courses in specific subjects: serious lectures of the type given in the university. This kind of course promotes culture and, furthermore, communicates a great deal of information to people.

Finally, the highest level of participation is achieved through active membership in professional circles and groups specializing in certain areas. Either working alone or in small groups, the individual under the supervision of experts can test his capacity in a new field and satisfy his inclinations in that direction.

The club as a social function clearly brings out people's inclinations and talents and helps some to acquire new professions by directing them to appropriate institutions (universities in the true sense).

Within the general framework of the club different subgroups can form to explore the basic areas of knowledge and activity existing in our society. For each basic area the club should have a section. How each section is further subdivided should vary and reflect the free and changing flow of interests among members.

A combination of permanence and fluidity in organization is absolutely necessary to preserve genuinely free relationships and to assure the individual both full choice of his pursuit and control of the way it develops.

Logically, too, we can suppose that every nucleus of enthusiasts, being a free and creative group, will need at least a core of five to nine members in order to function as we anticipate and multiples of this number to assure a maximum return on teamwork. Let us also suppose that in each of the ten sectors (eight fundamental fields, plus a section for collectors of stamps, coins, etc., and a sports section) there are about ten subdivisions. From our analysis we conclude that to obtain the desired free interaction and cultural vigor the club structure requires seven multiplied by ten, multiplied by ten again, that is, 700 active participants. These would then represent all the basic cultural activities current in our society.

Probability calculations based on the present educational level of our population and on the requirements of the proposed club structure indicate that the minimum population needed to create and sustain a complete club would be about 60,000 adults. This corresponds to a general population of about 100,000.

What will be the club's location in the urban plan? Where must it be built in order to be equally accessible to all of the 60,000 persons to whom it will be a real necessity? Its location in the period of transition to communism is of exceptional importance because, as leisure time and cultural demands increase, the club will tend more than any public function to attract great masses of people. The masses will spend as much of their time here as at home or at work.

The location of the club should take into consideration the fact of the population's continual movement during the workday and week. The working masses daily enter and leave the industrial complexes of an industrial zone, the agricultural enterprises of an agricultural zone, the centers and residential developments of the residential zone. Obviously the club's location should be determined by this triangle: residential area; service center; industrial complex. If we place the club in the service center or in the industrial complex, most people will have to make three instead of two trips per day. However, if the club is placed somewhere in the residential zone, most people will find it equally accessible.

It must be observed, moreover, that the social life of the masses—their gatherings and parades, their festivals and feasts—require a proper place and time. The place where the masses gather on great occasions (no matter how infrequently) should always, even when empty, express its high functional importance. It should be a permanent symbol of all the people's aspirations. Therefore, the place of assembly should be located with the club in a single architectural entity. Creating a center that would be equally accessible and of great public benefit to all could unify the whole residential zone.

The Unified Environment

As demonstrated earlier in our analysis, the aspects of community life that develop through free choice and association have their physical base partly in the club, which functions both as a center of cultural life and as a place for mass gatherings. This institution requires a supporting population of not fewer than 100,000. Cultural interests are, of course, pursued at home as well, and so leisure-time activity is directly connected with the residential system. Accordingly, the club and assembly hall are focal elements in the social structure of a large residential area.

As we contemplate the formation of freely developed groups, we recognize their great significance in planning the period of transition to communism. Requiring a minimum population of about 100,000 in order to flourish, the center of leisure-time activity becomes a decisive factor in planning, not only for its cultural initiative, but because it determines the population to be assigned to one entire residential area.

Thus the analysis of voluntary associations and activities leads us to conclusions that are analogous to those arrived at from analyzing how a primary residential complex should function in an urbanized area within an economic and geographic region.

In the last decade many city planners and sociologists have concentrated their interest on the enhanced role of the cultural center in urban life, anticipating that it will be a growing aspect of social life during the period of transition to communism.

These theoretical planners, although recognizing how vital a civic center is for stimulating cultural interests in an entire population, have concluded that capitalism does not encourage the kind of life that would find its expression in a civic center of this new type. Therefore, it is unlikely that it will be created in a capitalist environment.

Present bourgeois planning seems to justify this view. What tends to get built are shopping and entertainment centers.

The Social and Cultural Center

Our own urban-planning situation is in many respects analogous. In the years since the war we have generally constructed political and administrative centers. Beginning in the mid-fifties, a tendency to create shopping and entertainment centers became evident. As for the clubs, which have truly been hearths of culture since the very early years of the socialist revolution, neither their scale nor their social base is large enough to assure the desired intensity of communication and free interaction.

The proposals of Soviet planners and of the most progressive foreign architects do no more than insist on the value of such centers and two existing types of urban environment: the city and the small town.

No previous proposal has suggested that the cultural center, rather than industrial growth, should be the principal factor determining the size of a residential area. Yet industry, as we have shown in an earlier chapter, has no inherent significance that need determine the size of residential communities.

The question, on these new principles, is only how to relate increased industrial employment to a residential population whose size has been determined by its collective infrastructure.

The social center, which is based on free associations and common interests, constitutes the third (and largest) of the subdivisions of the total residential area, to which we would assign a population of about 100,000. In the framework of an urbanized complex of 100,000 persons, practically all the needs of the individual, whether related to his work or to his daily-life activities, can be served specifically.

To describe the residential area proposed by our plan we can hardly use the word "city." The breadth of that word and its many connotations would thoroughly confuse our inquiry. The term "city" has accumulated meanings throughout history and includes the notions of ancient, medieval, and early capitalist towns. According to our interpretation, it means collections of relatively small populations, which are concentrated compactly within a planned system of houses and streets. To employ the term "city" to designate a very different system comprising from 10,000 to 10,000,000 inhabitants is to interpret new and highly diversified phenomena in terms of old and rather inadequate conceptions, thus complicating our search for the structure of new urban environments.

The term "city," moreover, includes the notion of industrial life and industrial labor as well as highly developed cultural institutions. The use of this term always implies, therefore, that somewhere else there exist rural areas with a relatively low level of cultural and industrial activity. The important problem of ending the contrast of small town and city (especially vital at this point for our constructive reshaping of communism) is thereby ignored. The search for a single type of human environment would turn into merely elaborating and perfecting the traditional city.

For these reasons we have decided to invent a term, and so we have called the sociospatial complex examined in this chapter by a more complicated, yet, we think, a more precise name. We call it the **new unit of settlement** (NUS), thus underlining in the very name the significance of this entity as the basic sociospatial unit of a new society.

The spatial autonomy of the NUS, its system of residential sectors with a sociocultural center serving all the people, depends on a whole range of factors. We considered some of them before, when we were defining the physical plan: density, transportation,

The Plan of NUS (New Unit of Settlement)

and network of public services. Climate, topography, and, up to a point, the kind of economic production in which the majority of the population is engaged certainly also play a role in planning.

Improved health and sanitation in urban environments are presupposed for an intensive communal life. Planning of NUS should guarantee easy pedestrian access from every residential sector to both nature and the sociocultural center.

The opening of residential sectors to nature is particularly important. Most cities today, having developed in an unplanned way according to the traditional spoke plan, have sprawled beyond their original definition to the point where they join with unbroken stretches of built-up land spreading out for many miles. Therefore, to leave the city and find nature, it is necessary to take a trip for an hour or more by means of transportation.

We think that high standards of health and sanitation and of life in general can be achieved in an environment where all it takes to leave the built-up area is an easy walk. In other words, the limits of the whole area should be kept within the range of a twenty-minute walk. This means a mile can be considered a conventional distance from home to nature. The area covered by buildings should not be more than a mile from center to periphery.

If we start with this goal and with the dimensions of the massive and densely inhabited buildings required by NUS, we find that two basic plans, both providing good conditions for health and sanitation, can be used to relate the sectors to each other spatially. Let us examine them.

Linear arrangement: the sectors are stretched out along a single line; the school zone runs parallel to the residential one.

Circular arrangement: the sectors form a closed ring with an open space in the center; the school and sports area alternate with areas of residence.

Both these general schemes assure easy pedestrian access to nature and from that standpoint are equally desirable. In a concrete situation the choice of one or the other will obviously depend upon topography. The linear scheme is preferable where the residential sectors ought to be related in a certain way to prominent natural features, such as rivers, seacoast, or a great forest. The circular arrangement may prove impossible in areas where there are sharp drops in terrain, or under special atmospheric or climatic conditions.

The linear scheme may also prove the more reasonable when a great part of the NUS population is active in a kind of economic production that does not need to be segregated from the residential area. Here we would logically wish to create the possibility of direct transit between home and work. Unfortunately, in the linear plan the various residential sectors are bound to be unequally distant from the sociocultural center. The end units will be at a maximum distance of two miles from the center and so will need motorized transportation to reach it.

With the circular plan, on the other hand, the center of NUS is equidistant from all the residential units and is accessible to everyone by an approximately equal walk (the radius of NUS will not surpass 1.2 miles). Unequal distance of the residential units from the sociocultural center is one disadvantage of the linear scheme. To some extent, however, it can be compensated by a very direct and economical system of transportation.

The growth of free associations among people, particularly those based on leisure-time activities, and the tendency for units of production to be placed at a distance from residential areas indicate that the NUS conforming to a circular plan will become the most common type.

Comparative schemes for the planning of residential areas: (1) traditional city: central area distant from nature; peripheral sectors distant from center; (2) linear schema: the built-up zone of a depth of 1.5 kilometers would extend for about 6 kilometers to house a population of 100,000; residential sectors ideally enjoy equal proximity to nature, but the peripheral sectors are more distant from the center; (3) circular schema with central green mass; residential sectors are pleasantly linked to nature and are equally convenient to nature and the center.

Accordingly, the residential portion of the new urban environment becomes an autonomous space, complete in itself and clearly defined. The plan for NUS as a static projection (not incorporating the feature of growth) becomes a clear and integral part of the dynamic context of any economic and geographic region.

STRUCTURE OF THE URBAN

ENVIRONMENT

The chaotic growth of cities will be replaced by a dynamic system of urban settlement. This system will evolve out of an integrated and self-sufficient nucleus: the NUS.

Urban growth, through the formation of nuclei, represents a new phase in the conscious development of urban life. The goal is to transform the whole planet into a unified sociological environment.

NUS is the fundamental unit of that organism. It is the "quantum" of the urban environment, the finite unit, limited by itself and directing itself.

The realization of the projected NUS can be initiated today, for its real economic and technical infrastructure already exists.

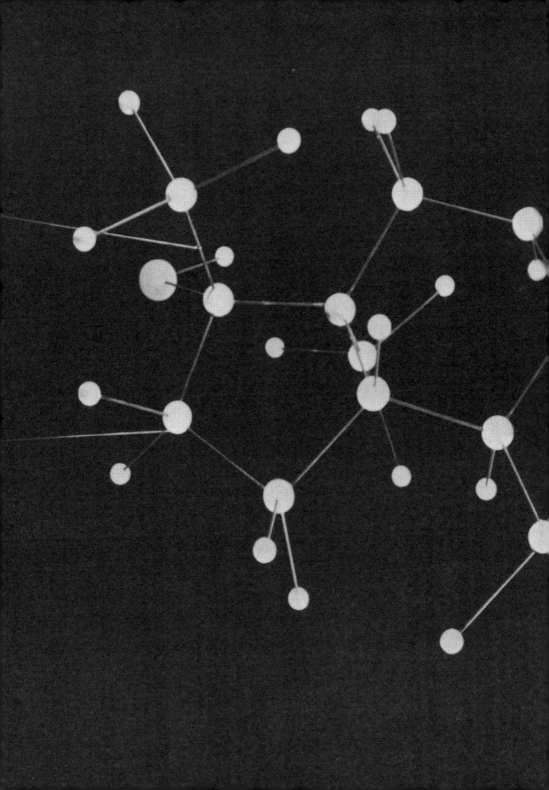

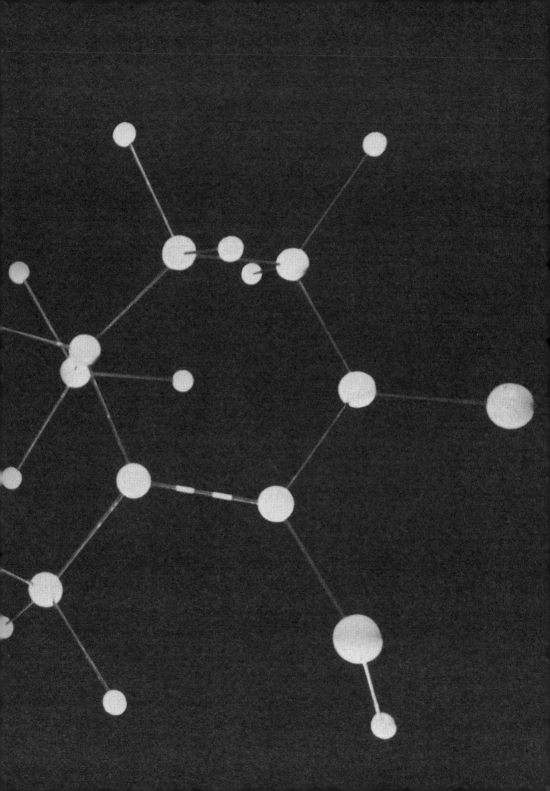

We must apply to the unified and constructive plan of communist urban life the results of our inquiry concerning various aspects of its functional structure. To make our model more understandable we shall complete our argument by presenting some specific plans and suggesting some ways of realizing the functional structure that we have previously described on an abstract level. These schemes will inevitably appear to be rather conventional, lacking the depth and the concrete detail proper to an architectural project, but this defect, in our opinion, is outweighed by the usefulness of the schemes in clearly illustrating our fundamental hypothesis.

Demographic expansion, including the rapid industrial transformation of territories rich in natural resources, as well as the never-ending expansion in partly developed areas and the tendency of heavy industry and scientific centers to take over vast land areas all give us reason to anticipate some unified form for the urban environment, a form in which there is close interdependence of environmental elements (industrial, scientific, and residential) and in which compact regions are created for their intensive development.

The emergence of rationally planned areas many miles in dimension indicates that we have moved into a new stage of conscious urban development ultimately aimed at uniting the planet into a single system corresponding to a new kind of social organization and to the growing potential of modern technology.

The region of urban settlement with many nuclei

The System of Urban Growth According to the Formation of Nuclei

Diagram of group
distribution in the urban
environment

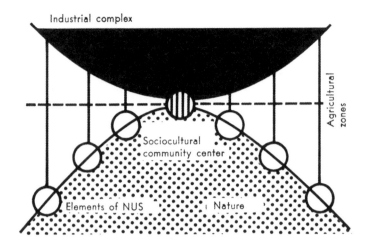

Industrial complex

Agricultural zones

Sociocultural
community center

Elements of NUS   Nature

can become populated by as many as several million
people. The region itself is formed by the economic
interdependence of its development, from the industrial complex to the industrial area and the industrial
region. The region has a single system of transportation, a centralized administration, and a unified
system of education and research.

The urban nuclei in this region form a system that
is spatially autonomous although connected with industrial areas, auxiliary and agricultural lands, and
areas preserved in their natural state.

Each unit of settlement (NUS) is planned to have
a standard social and spatial structure and to fulfill
independently the major cultural needs and services
for its inhabitants. The fact of standardization does
not exclude diversity, however, in the local planning
situation, which should respond to topography, climate, and other indigenous factors.

These units of settlement (NUS), novel in their size
and conception, would be rationally distributed
through an urban zone. They should be planned fairly
far apart (from one to two diameters of a single NUS)
in order to keep (or create) large green belts between
them, which could be directly contiguous with the

residential areas. The natural conditions in the green belts between different NUS could provide recreational services, including institutions for public health and sport for the entire population of the administrative zone. Other unused land areas in the zones assigned to settlement could be given over to agriculture, thereby serving the population with fresh produce and providing the food industry with raw material. A large portion of the population living in the NUS could be employed in these activities. It is likely also that many people in the urbanized area would be attracted into agricultural labor during their leisure periods. Consequently, the weblike structure of urbanized zones that results from our planning of nuclei will largely abolish the distinction between rural and urban environments.

Every zone with its urban nuclei will require some centralized institutions to co-ordinate and direct its economic activity and scientific education. These institutions can be placed in a single complex located at the center of the whole urbanized area, where, along with administrative offices to direct scientific research and higher education, a center for economic co-ordination would be located. Here, too, significantly, there can be an information center on which the sociocultural activities of the NUS, including its political and administrative functions, can depend.

The regions with settlements of nuclei, therefore, would be free of many of the serious defects that are characteristic of existing gigantic urban agglomerations with their histories of unplanned growth, health and sanitation problems, remoteness from nature, tangled transportation, and unequal access to both center and periphery. At the same time, the urban zone that is based on nuclei will preserve all the real virtues of the contemporary metropolis, especially the high level of social and cultural life.

The residential zone, attached economically to an

Diagram of NUS in an
agricultural zone.
Along the radial links of
transportation transient
communities are housed
in mobile homes.

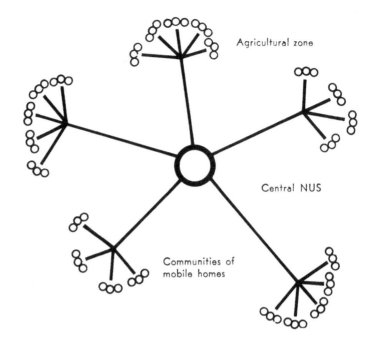

Agricultural zone

Central NUS

Communities of
mobile homes

evolving industrial complex, will form part of a total
economic and geographic region and will call for an
administrative and territorial organization related to
it. In a single economic and geographic region one
or several nuclei could develop, where most of the
region's population would be concentrated. The
center of one of these would presumably take over
the co-ordinating and directing of the whole region.

In the process of spreading to new land areas, a
single NUS or small groups of two or three may arise.
In time, these will split off into autonomous regions
or be united with neighboring regions, depending on
the economic and geographic characteristics of the
territory.

New NUS, isolated and relatively autonomous,
very remote from all others, will probably arise quite
often in agrarian zones, at centers for the processing
of agricultural products. Similar isolated settlements
will tend to appear around refineries in mining areas.

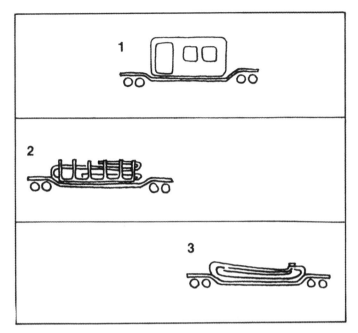

Complex of mobile homes for temporary settlements in agricultural and mining areas: (1) homes; (2) complex of facilities provided; (3) public building of pneumatic type.

In these cases NUS will be the social, administrative, and cultural center for a widely scattered population.

If such a central NUS can be linked by adequate means of transportation with the agricultural or mining area as a whole, it will make sense to construct temporary housing (perhaps mobile homes) for seasonal use by agricultural workers (or for miners rotating periods of work in the mines).

What we have said concerning new areas of settlement leads us to sketch out a method for reconstructing existing urban areas as well. Reconstruction always touches on a great number of previously developed situations and cannot be really resolved unless one knows all the details and has worked out a full and accurate plan. Reconstruction cannot be achieved by blindly following some simple formula or a single plan. This is a problem that calls for unique and often surprising approaches. But we may briefly suggest here some helpful principles.

109

Diagram indicating to what extent a city could be reconstructed. The undifferentiated system of neighborhoods is divided by green open spaces into large nuclear urban areas, each with its autonomous center.
Industrial zones are indicated by the open space above.

Where there are concentrations of millions of people, we want to make a gradual transition from the metropolis to the urbanized zone composed of NUS nuclei. We want to intersperse green belts through existing complexes of buildings, to transform the whole into a system of large civic units (type NUS), each with its administrative, cultural, scientific, and educational center.

In small and medium-size cities where the possibility exists for intensive economic development, it can be stimulated by the construction of new NUS, which also would raise the level of consumer and cultural services. On the other hand, if economic development is slow, the logical procedure would be to remove the population gradually to the nearest urban center.

In agricultural regions economic activity, including modern agricultural work and cultural life, can begin to cluster at physically and economically advantageous locations. There should eventually develop at these locations a central NUS, or group of NUS, whose cultural institutions would attract the population of these regions.

The basis of our planning is the concept of a new unit of settlement (NUS); we propose a "quantum" for urbanization, the size of which can vary only within narrow limits. This is a theoretically valid premise and merits a supplementary word of explanation.

In defining the average numerical size of NUS populations at 100,000, we do not mean this to be a fixed or rigid total. It may indeed be argued that because of an elaborate complex of local conditions there might be a NUS in some places with a population of 150,000, or twin NUS of 200,000, sharing a single enlarged sociocultural center.

Although we are assuming that further experimental inquiry into the nature and growth of free sociocultural life will lead to corrections of our projections, we nevertheless do postulate NUS as always representing the fundamental unit of the future community. We also maintain that a population of 100,000 accurately reflects the correlation between optimum size of a large primary residential unit and the requirements of an organizational structure that will support intensive free association and the pursuit of cultural interests.

It is important to clarify how the "maximum" size we have set for the population and dimensions of any NUS will fit in with the requirements of economic production, especially where there is vast economic growth.

In contemporary production it is common practice to isolate certain essential activities from the fundamental process of manufacturing. (These include administration, experimentation, research, and programming.) This is done regardless of whether employment is increasing or declining. The procedure in either case directly affects what happens in the urban environment.

While the most important manufacturing processes show a tendency to move away from residential areas, administrative and research activities that are directly connected with them appear to be gravitating toward urban centers.

A system of rapid transportation connects NUS, the industrial area, and the scientific center, unifying the whole urbanized region. Thus it is possible to distribute the labor force with equal efficiency over the whole region and regulate the immigration of people into an urbanized region in addition to its normal population expansion by settling all persons in new units of settlement (NUS).

Sometimes a single NUS will form an adjunct to a particular industrial complex or to certain intensively developed sectors of an industrial zone because these still employ a major portion of the population. Even then, however, there is no reason for NUS to differ radically, either in physical size or in population density, from the proposed dimensions.

Although the location of some industries is determined by proximity to refineries, mines, and such operations, other manufacturing processes can be located practically anywhere in a region as long as they are reasonably related to the overall transportation and production system.

When a great number of industries, each requiring spatial autonomy, move into an urban region, it is easy to imagine that an isolated industry of minimal dimensions will bring in a certain number of people, say 11,000, while larger industries will bring in proportionally more.

The development of the urban environment on a regional scale will, of course, be simultaneous with the construction of NUS nuclei. Therefore, we can begin to envision the urban environment of the future as a dynamic system, one in which the number of elements expands rationally in the process of development. Each element, however, is not planned to expand autonomously but to be integrated with a growing quantity of other elements into an expanding system. The concept is analogous to the growth process in nature by which each element is assured an appropriate site and function. The growth of any complex organism has a definite limit, after which the organism generates a new organism resembling itself. The chaotic growth of the modern city beyond any limits is comparable only to the growth of a malignant tumor. This kind of growth prevents the normal activity of the organism and ultimately destroys it.

The idea of limiting the growth of the community is nothing new in itself. The literature on urban planning in capitalist societies is full of good intentions for ending the monstrous expansion of metropolitan

"Continuity and discontinuity: two contradictory features linked indissolubly together, and found generally in natural, social, and mental phenomena."—Bolsaja Sovetskaja Enciklopedija, XXXIV, 434.

113

areas. Given their social context, however, these ideas, no matter how reasonable, are impossible to put into practice.

In Soviet planning the idea of limiting community growth has long been part of a fairly widespread concept: the concept of the "ideal city." This concept begins with the attempt to proportion the groups within an urban population numerically in order to assure the best economic and social development, hygienic conditions, and transportation, and generally to solve the major urban problems.

The very term "ideal city" implies that these problems (and especially the problem of the organic relationship between production, housing, and long-range economic planning) are all to be resolved within the framework of a single integral urban complex, while the study of the relation between environment and large-scale industry is relegated to the background. This intellectual starting point leads to irreconcilable contradictions. For one thing, the population size of the "ideal city" is rigidly set and cannot accommodate the massive influx of population attracted by rapid industrial expansion. This population size is not based on any one real consideration, moreover, but is simply a kind of arithmetical average among several answers to different and separate problems.

Our notion of a new basic element in the urban environment derives from quite a different perspective, one which takes the whole urbanized region into account. This means that we can fully anticipate industrial growth and can study and predict the effects of economic and transportation systems on the total industrial and territorial complex.

We have arrived at a clear and secure position for defining a self-regulating basic unit. Our new element in the urban environment (NUS) was not postulated on the basis of factors extrinsic to it but on the basis of the urban residential situation itself, in other words, on the basis of the real individual and social requirements of communist society.

We have attempted to describe the functional structure of the urban environment by presenting all the data that have a direct bearing on the kind of buildings to be constructed and on their planned relationships. It is necessary now to sketch, at least briefly, some architectural solutions that would be possible within this framework and to consider some of the available construction techniques.

We must turn from our inquiry into the social matrix to some general architectural schemes that, although general, are much less abstract than the theoretical arguments and statistics that we have been presenting so far. To speak concretely, we must consider how long a time period we expect it will take to move from plan to actuality. The rhythm of progress today is highly accelerated, and the period of time that we estimate defines from the planners' point of view a stage in technological and economic development—a level of technical innovation.

New techniques in architecture open exciting possibilities. The use of synthetic insulation materials is bringing major improvements to building. We can predict, for example, that a plastic film will soon replace glass as the usual window material. Combined with the new, but already praticable, concept of inflatable structures, this means that whole complexes of residential buildings can be enclosed and given an artificial climate. There are unlimited possibilities in the use of effective substitutes for primitive methods of construction, methods that have only traditional value. Construction is becoming a field for fascinating experiments.

From Plan to Actuality

Time will change the appearance of the new city to the point of unrecognizability. The use of laminated transparent plastics may lead to the creation of fantastic cities under transparent domes. The eventual development of bearing structures of metal and reinforced concrete will probably make the city of the future take on the character of a single gigantic edifice.

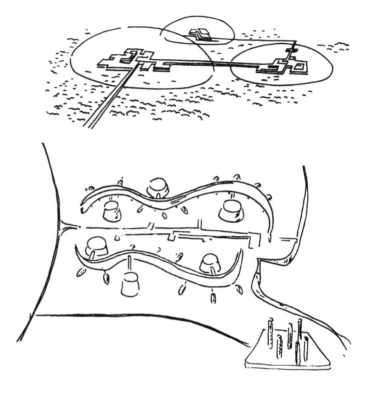

In this book we have avoided fantasies about the distant future; we have tried to show how a new functional structure for the urban environment is already possible. To use this planning approach as the basis for spatial solutions would in itself generate a qualitatively new environment. The proposals we mention in this chapter should not be compared with the innumerable existing proposals for an architecture of the future. Our proposals are intended only to clarify the principles to be applied to certain new urban projects. We are absolutely not engaged in looking for new kinds of building materials or techniques; those we describe are quite conventional construction techniques that are normal today, or ones that will be common in the next few decades.

Our plans for NUS illustrate no more than our general conception of its spatial arrangement. We certainly do not intend to dictate the actual profile of a settlement or the design of any individual building. We realize, moreover, that every environmental improvement is made not only by building new structures but by relating these in some way to existing surroundings. Any plan we offer, therefore, even the most abstract, assumes that change will be gradual, consisting of increments of progress toward a distant goal.

The standards for areas and cubic space that we have applied here to NUS are ones that will actually be guiding construction for the next few years. The accelerated building program and the progressive rise in standards for housing and public services that appear here simply conform to our society's actual present plans.

Accordingly, to comprehend our examples, one must realize that our standards are the ones actually expected to prevail in the near future.

The fundamental principles governing the NUS:

Space Planning

1. Equal mobility for all. Residential sectors are at equal walking distance from the center and from the forests and parks surrounding them.

2. Distances are planned on a pedestrian scale. No home is so remote from the center or from the park area that it cannot be reached by a reasonably short walk.

3. Elimination of danger from vehicular traffic. Rapid public transportation operates outside the pedestrian area yet is linked centrally with NUS. (Its circuits carry people from home to work and from home to home.)

4. Green belts. Every sector is surrounded on at least two sides by open land.

Diagram of NUS.
1. Residential units
2. School and sports area
3. Rapid transport above
   pedestrian level
4. Highway
5. Community center of
   NUS

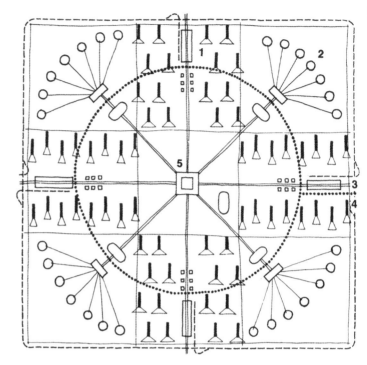

Diagram of the NUS. The plan of the NUS here presented assumes typical conditions: the NUS is in an urban zone with nuclei; it is shown in a geographically central and average region; the sectors are arranged on a circular plan with no topographical breaks. What we indicate here is the most abstract projection of NUS and the clearest illustration of its basic structure. This plan is simultaneously a symbol of the idea and a program for its realization.

Residential Sector

Sectors are planned like spokes around the NUS center, which focuses attention on the large community park and on the sociocultural center. These together occupy an area of 200 acres. Residential sectors are linked to each other and to the industrial complexes located three to four miles away by a system of public transportation. Motorized traffic circulates on a peripheral highway, except for a throughroad that takes it into the center. Roads branching from this one provide access to, but do not traverse, residential, educational, and recreational areas.

The basic concept stresses:
1. A pedestrian scale. The distance from any resi-

dence to the center of services including public transportation will not exceed 500 yards to 600 yards (a seven-minute walk).

2. The school environment. Placing the school community at the edge of a residential area allows the schoolgrounds to connect directly with park and forest lands.

3. Parks and recreational land. Spaces between the residential sectors will be green, linking the trees and landscaping of the center to forests and parks outside the developed area.

The residential sector is a densely built-up area and includes sixteen primary complexes. It is surrounded by a green belt, at least one quarter of a mile wide, and it incorporates a shopping center for 25,000 persons, some light industry, and space for collective activities.

Storage space for both residential and nonresidential buildings is provided by basements. Underground access is also planned for delivery and other services coming from the peripheral road. This means that all heavy traffic can be kept out of the center, which will contain only light pavilions reached by a wide walkway. In this central area, close to shops and services, we locate the subway or elevated station.

There is enough space between two residential sectors to provide for a school community and areas for recreation, rest, and sports. Set among fields and gardens, the school community has a three-story central residence, around which are clustered various educational buildings. Four of these are sufficient to begin with. Later, in response to the growing educational system, this number will have to increase. For the present, however, school structures will appear, as shown in our diagram, bordering on the outer area of green, where general sports facilities and an indoor swimming pool are also developed, to serve both

1

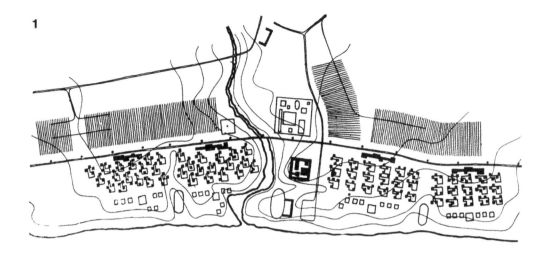

The diagram of NUS does not dictate a single unique spatial solution. Despite the fact of a single functional structure, the profile of each settlement will be modified by various concrete circumstances, by the creative character of the architect, and by the effective level of technology being applied.
1. An example of linear arrangement of residential units near nonharmful industrial plants. High-rise buildings with tower, some of which are united with a block containing shared services, will form the basic residential units.
2. Example of compact arrangement of residential units. Buildings of six to nine floors are primary residential units.
The urban total:
1. Primary residential units
2. Community center for the sector

2

students and adults. Medical and general health services should be available here.

The geometry and physical size of the residential sector can be described in other ways. The sector may be viewed as a planned high-rise area with two extensions for school and sports, or it can be identi-

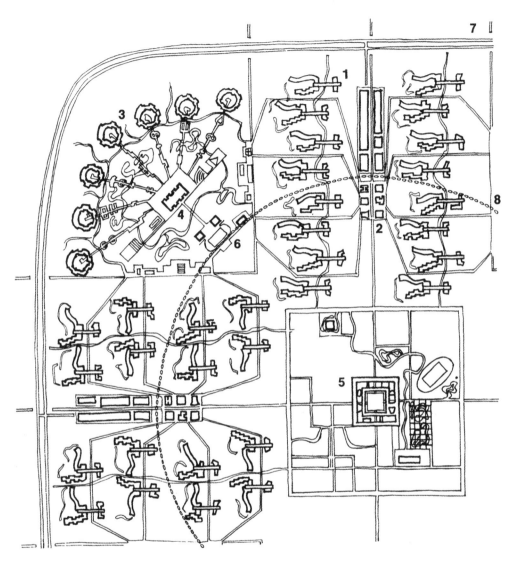

3. School community complex
4. Academic center
5. Community center of NUS
6. Sports complex
7. Highway
8. Rapid transport above pedestrian level

fied as a school campus and sports area with two densely populated residential extensions. From either point of view, our plan shows an integrated system of housing, consumer services, schools, and recreational facilities for 25,000 inhabitants.

3. School community
   complex
4. Academic center
5. Community center of
   NUS
6. Sports complex
7. Highway
8. Rapid transport above
   pedestrian level

Primary Residential Unit

The principles underlying our plan for housing units are:

1. Reasonable economy, privacy, and comfort. To answer these needs, high-rise residential structures are combined with low-rise children's institutions.

2. Variation in total structures based on the combination of standard units. The basic apartment unit

Primary residential unit:
1. Seen from above
2. Residential cell
The area of auxiliary installations is shaded. The vertical connecting link (elevator, stairs) is indicated by a circle.

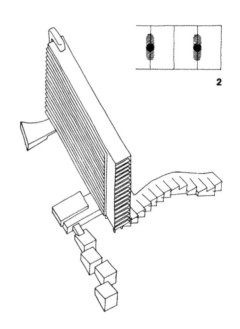

2

serves as a module, and combinations can be varied to create apartments of different types to suit different numbers of persons per family.

3. Bilateral orientation is recommended for all types of apartments except those for single persons.

The primary residential complex includes seventeen-story apartment blocks, some primary consumer services, and a low-rise preschool and elementary school.

In the high-rise building both vertical traffic (elevators) and horizontal communication (mezzanines) are necessary. The system of mezzanines assures a higher level of comfort and privacy than do corridors.

In practice, many variations of the mezzanine concept are possible. Our diagram indicates only the general location of elevators and stairs and assumes that the details would depend on the specific construction plan. The first floor of housing is raised above ground level to make the building independent of terrain and to avoid blocking pedestrian traffic.

Consumer services can be provided wherever desired on the lower floors of the residential structure.

In planning the apartments we have taken account of the auxiliary areas. Elevators, stairs, bathroom facilities, and kitchens for two apartments form a single compact module. By locating all the mechanical services in one area, installation and repairs are made much easier. All apartments (except those on the mezzanine floors) have a bilateral orientation.

Within the two-apartment module, housing can be carved out for three, four, or five persons. Apartments for one and two persons are placed on the mezzanines; those for six or more persons in penthouses. Hence our residential unit can include a range of apartments, based on the prevailing norm of about 100 square feet per person for private living area, and in line with the demographic composition of our population. In our plan of a typical apartment layout, we have kept in mind how it can be modified for different area ratios or in relation to eventual changes in demand.

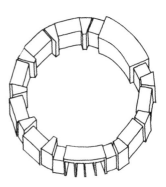

School Community
Complex

Our present system allows us to house up to 1,750 persons in one high-rise building. If the space allowance per person increases while the system of public education continues to expand, the number of permanent residents occupying the same building area will decrease to perhaps 1,000 adults, and this process of decongestion will increase the space per resident.

Primary schools with dormitories will have a gen-

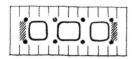

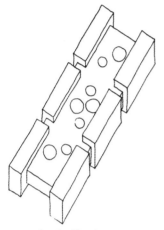

Academic Center
Shopping Center

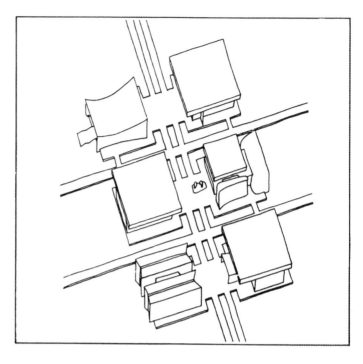

eral service area with dining room and kitchen, gym and classroom space, administrative and teachers' offices, and first aid station. The children's dormitories are to be built around this central service unit. Each dormitory will be self-contained and will have its own access to the garden. The dormitories will be linked, however, to each other and to the central service unit. Bathrooms, auxiliary facilities, playrooms, and bedrooms must be planned in each separate dormitory.

As the system of public education grows, new buildings will be needed. The preschool and elementary-school population in each primary residential complex will eventually require twelve dormitories.

Secondary-School Community

Two basic components are required by these schools: classroom buildings and dormitories. For the secondary-school community we propose a circular

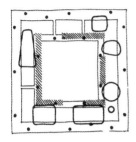

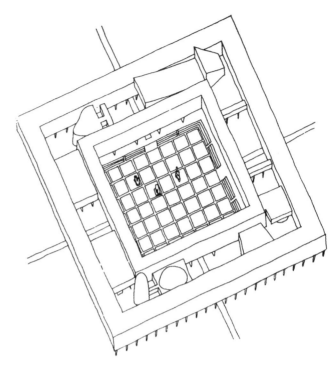

three-story structure surrounding a large courtyard. Community Center of NUS
On the ground floor: classrooms, recreation rooms,
living rooms with easy access to the street. On the
upper floors: dormitories and communal rooms for
living. In the first phase of construction the second-
and third-floor recreation rooms with separate en-
trances can be used for classrooms. The circular continuum of this scholastic building is broken at two
places: (1) the open passageway into the courtyard;
(2) an area of small sports facilities and teachers'
rooms. By placing these two breaks where there is
least sunlight, sun in the classrooms can be maximized.

The main educational building is a long structure
three stories high. Along its façades, we locate laboratories, bathrooms, classrooms, and recreational
rooms. In the center, illuminated by skylights, are the
library and four large auditoriums. On the first floor
are the entrance halls with closets and the special

125

laboratories. The whole building (because of shifting times of use by different groups) can serve 3,000 persons.

The Proposed Consumer Service Center

This center of the residential sector is composed of pavilions surrounding an elevated plaza. Areas under this platform are reserved for storage rooms, workshops, and auxiliary facilities, all served by a centralized delivery, shipping, and waste-disposal system. Based upon projections of future services, two pavilions are planned for shops, while another four are designated respectively for a cinema to seat 800, a restaurant, the sector administration unit, and community services.

The construction of the center can be planned in stages. Our diagrammatic plan indicates additional sports facilities, including an outdoor swimming pool and an indoor stadium. These functions are intended to develop along with others in the community center, like the general clinic and other medical institutions. All of these represent components that would eventually create a unified system of public facilities and services for the residential area.

Proposed Social and Cultural Center for the Whole Community

This center occupies a special place in the social and physical plan of NUS. It appears in our sketches as a building with three levels. The ground floor contains only the courtyard with its public access. The second level above the courtyard is an open square, the sides designed as two narrow bands containing a variety of facilities. The exterior band includes two-story galleries alternating with single-story studios, seminar rooms, and classrooms, while the interior band overlooking the courtyard would contain reading rooms, archives, small individual studios, and labs.

Between these two bands, larger units, such as assembly halls, two theaters, a planetarium, a large gymnasium, and a swimming pool could be freely

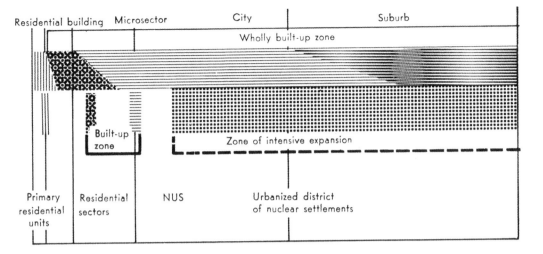

| Residential building | Microsector | City | Suburb |

Wholly built-up zone

Built-up zone

Zone of intensive expansion

| Primary residential units | Residential sectors | NUS | Urbanized district of nuclear settlements |

Present and future structure of the urban environment. The elements of the functional structure are quite precisely differentiated in the present urban environment. Among these the dominant one is the residential building, hence the microsector (that is, a sector of about 30,000 to 40,000 population), and the city itself, with a population range of 10,000 to several million. Under existing conditions, the microsector and even the city appear as uninterrupted built-up areas with small green patches. This kind of development in agglomerations of over 100,000 population produces unsatisfactory living conditions. The accompanying table shows the significance of our proposal. The elements of the functional structure are clearly distinguished: primary residential unit and urbanized unit, replacing respectively the residential building and the microsector of a population, whatever its size. NUS, with a population of 100,000, constitutes a nucleus of the city. An agglomeration of any size can be restructured in this way, with the total population distributed in residential units and NUS. Conversely, areas of uninterrupted natural expanse can contain no more than one NUS. Instead of gigantic cities, here is the urban district organized by nuclei and linked to a system of industrial production. The tables given here show clearly the difference in principle between the continuous structure of the existing environment and the discontinuous structure of the urban environment of the future.

In the existing environment the fundamental unit of growth is the microsector; but this is a unit without a constant size and often shaped by the accidental pressures of local conditions. In the anticipated structure the fundamental unit of growth is NUS, a clearly defined social and spatial complex.

located. These could be connected where convenient to the working spaces in the parallel bands. Our sketch of this building designates each side of the square for one of the four fundamental fields of cultural activity: science and technology, crafts, the arts, and sports. Since planning and construction needs will vary, however, the form obviously must be flexible, and it certainly is not easy to foresee how this community and social center would be affected by voluntary associations and the pursuit of individual interests. New economic possibilities undoubtedly will affect the center's outcome, too.

Our diagrams should be sufficient, however, to show that we can really create an urban environment that meets individual and social needs, even while working within the present phase of transition to communism, and that we can base our building plans on the existing economic infrastructure. Thus this prototype design could be realized today merely by taking advantage of the technical possibilities and functional organization of contemporary architecture.

THE PHYSICAL UNITY OF THE NUS

(NEW UNIT OF SETTLEMENT)

The new architecture represents an inevitable and innovative evolution out of past building traditions. The rationality of this architecture and its use of space derive from the basic "plastic" reality of the surrounding world. The physical planning of the new city reflects the harmony and integrated character of its social structure.

A unified planning approach assigns to each element a role in the formation of human environments. The future belongs to an architecture that is permeated with the spirit of organic synthesis.

This chapter attempts to show how the new planning science, which is based on sociospatial concepts of the urban environment, influences architecture, or more precisely, the language of architecture. During the past several decades, planners have been trying to arrive at a master plan for environments, which could handle all the contingencies of unplanned growth. Now a spatial system that corresponds with and satisfies the needs of all men is being sought. This search, unique to our time, has assigned a new role to architecture and new tasks that cannot be accomplished by older methods. Neither the possibilities nor the limitations of new methods were at all clear at first, but after persistent attempts to apply them, planners have begun to recognize their usefulness and can now discuss them on the basis of experience or as familiar ideas.

The work of an architect can be called contemporary only if he understands how and why in his time the goals and techniques of architecture have changed. Changes have not come by chance. We may come to understand the logic of the process if we examine the basic stages by which traditional European architecture has evolved. Even very unusual aspects of the new architecture are transitional events in an unceasing evolution. Attempts to obstruct this process of change must yield to the realization of its inevitability and to an understanding of the way in which change is radically reshaping past traditions.

Initially, the building activities of man grew out of the need to shelter human life by abstracting a suit-

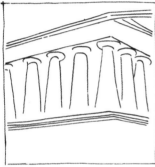  

The faceted mass of the temple sparkling in the sun stands out against the background of nature. As soon as it can be seen from a great distance, it attracts full attention, like a sail on the horizon, like a gleaming jewel. The landscape slowly opens up, like the palm of a hand holding a white crystal. The temple comes into view. The varied surface of its façades becomes more visible; details assume relief and show their complex and rhythmic structure. Finally, there is a moment when the building fills the whole visual field with a complex play of lines and forms.

able artificial space from the world of nature. Accordingly, one of the first achievements of architecture was its ability to enclose human existence in a space, the limits of which were determined by the functions taking place in that space.

This concept of space has evolved continually since the first clear architectural expression was given to it in ancient Greece. The temple was the first public building of antiquity to reflect a fully conscious architectural typology. As a building form it expresses a few simple and widely accepted functional principles. These principles subordinate a whole group of spaces to a single comprehensive structural order.

As a visual form the temple appears in relief against the city and stands clearly distinct from the rest of the environment. The sea, the sky, and the mountains serve as its backdrop. Whether it tops the natural line of a hill or sets the scale of a valley the

Greek temple relates to, but is set apart from, nature. By its severe geometry it expresses man's capacity to create a rational human order.

Atlhough the temple is planned to relate to its surroundings, it clearly contrasts with them. By being a focal element in the landscape, it dominates the entire spatial composition. Not only does the temple subordinate surrounding spatial relationships; it also gives an orientation to all views to the world outside as well.

Man's ability to perceive spatial impressions is not unlimited; he can take in only a limited number of diverse elements simultaneously without fatigue. This tolerance sets his maximum perceptual intake.

If a building's complexity does not exceed this limit, its composition can be perceived as a whole. Otherwise, its visual identity becomes lost in a flux of diverse, unrelated impressions.

In the same way, a mass of details can spoil a painting. We instinctively move away from the canvas to create conditions for better perception. As our awareness of details diminishes, we are able to experience the painting's total impact.

Actually, many distinct elements can be comprehended with maximum perception, provided that the elements are grouped in rhythmic sequences. The Greek temple is such a structure, perceivable as an integrated composition from several interrelated reference points.

The monolithic stone architecture of the Greeks, combined with their highly developed craftsmanship in its detailing, enabled the artisans to give the simple geometrical space a rich complexity. This makes the process of perception a varied and profound experience, never disrupting, however, the force and beauty of the total composition.

Alternating the elements of the Greek orders (capitols, columns, metopes, etc.) produced harmonious spatial rhythms. Completing and reinforcing each other, they make up a visual language that can wholly articulate the building's elemental mass.

<table>
<tr><td>

Architectural Typologies

</td><td>

From the demonstrated increase in material resources through history and the experience of social and political change, architecture has come to include an ever greater number of typologies.

Architecture was called upon to create models for the daily existence of a feudal elite and later of a dominant bourgeoisie. A luxurious kind of building developed, centering on palaces and mansions. Working for his patron's excessive individual needs, however, the architect was forced to isolate heterogeneous spaces to the point where they could no longer be integrated within one environmental system. Buildings, for the most part, became totally unrelated to each other and to their own interior functions.

The medieval city is an exciting agglomerate of buildings. It was not meant to be perceived through the unfolding rhythms of classical Greek architecture. Man experienced the city as a set of broken spatial fragments, each requiring separate acts of perception. The cathedral or palace became the dominant element that was needed to tie these fragments together.

The architects of classical antiquity tried to place their monumental structures on open sites in order to make them visible from all sides and therefore perceivable in an integrated spatial composition. Renaissance architects made particular use of perspectives created by giving direction to narrow and enclosed views. Powerful cornices also gave an ordered rhythm to street façades.

The building methods and uses of materials that were harmoniously related in the monumental Greek architecture became diffused during the medieval

</td></tr>
</table>

Rhythm is a creative means in composition. In the two photographs shown here the number of objects is the same: above, chaos, undifferentiated agglomeration; below, the fundamental rhythmic elements of a composition are clearly displayed.

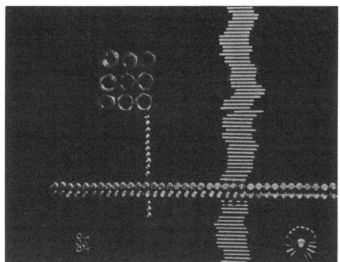

period. The structure of buildings and their façades were designed separately.

During the neoclassic era, gigantic palaces developed, and even whole building systems were organized on the basis of a rigorous architectural and planning hierarchy. The architect was seeking to unify a complex composition by using a single visual con-

The medieval town appears as the combination of an infinite number of different architectural compositions. Verticality, dominating the town, focuses this variety of scenes and orients the space as a whole.

cept, and this demanded a maximum use of perceptual powers. Spatial rhythms were created not by single elements but by articulating entire façades. Varying the design of façades by making progressive changes in architectural orders, from Renaissance to neoclassic, became the major esthetic concern of architecture.

Throughout this period the bearing wall remained the fundamental structural principle. In the early Renaissance the bearing-wall concept combined the need for a barrier against climate and the need for social separation. Many expressive innovations developed in the use of materials and methods of construction. In time, though, the wall developed into a screen to hide the building and came to have, therefore, only a decorative function.

Despite its lace of structural function, the decorated façade, with its ordered elements, continued to maintain esthetic prominence as long as architecture and planning focused all attention on a few monumental building types.

As building demands have expanded, however, to meet the needs of greater numbers of people, the contradiction between highly individuated building and a rigid canon of spatial esthetics has grown ever clearer and more irreconcilable. But without materials superior to stone and brick, architecture was held to compromise solutions.

A critical period came at the beginning of the twentieth century. Building expansion and technological innovations introduced industrial processes into construction. Architecture changed its emphasis to functional solutions and logical procedures. Steel and reinforced concrete became generally used. Efficient insulating materials were developed. Variations of color and form in the façade no longer depended upon the building's structural system.

At last, construction methods no longer limit the

The new building, a structure made of light and green.

freedom and independence of architectural expression. Traditional canons and formalistic approaches no longer apply. The road is wide open. Several decades of experience, moreover, have given contemporary architecture the capacity to articulate clearly, if not to answer completely, the major new problems.

Geometry and Design

After the excessive mannerism of the nineteenth century, an architecture based on concrete and glass, with a simplicity and ascetic rigor, has developed. Representing a revolutionary phase in the history of architecture, it demonstrates a new relationship to technology. Now construction becomes a branch of industrial production. Unity and the repetition of homogeneous elements are demanded both by new visual conditions and the urgent need for mass-produced housing. The new concept of housing concentrates upon light and open spaces; the courtyard with its well no longer blocks out open horizons. Instead of

Ornament has no function in the façade of the contemporary building. It reappears in the immediate area of public visibility, along the sidewalk, where the human scale dominates.

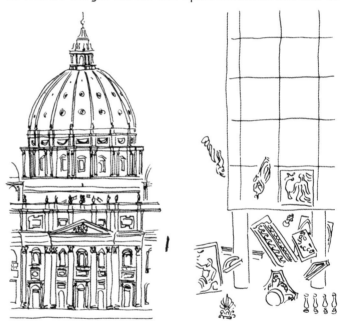

façades on the street, or monumental piazzas, we now open our residential buildings to panoramic views.

Previously, full visual attention was concentrated on a single building. Now it is given to the whole visual field that a viewer experiences. That field takes in the whole urban environment.

140

The single building relates to an elaborate spatial complex, as a column relates to an ancient temple. It becomes part of a whole, a rhythmic element, a note in a harmony.

Façades can be seen in their totality only from a great distance. Therefore, detailed ornamentation is superfluous, even harmful, since it tends to produce confusion and break up fundamental building rhythms.

The visual simplicity of façades and the rhythmic massing of identical elements are both basic preoccupations of the new architecture. Within its framework

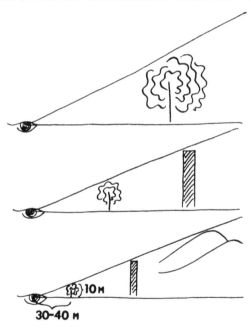

Zones of near and distant viewing. The dimensions of the near zone are defined by the possibility of detailed perception of plastic variety—color and shape—in objects. In practice, the zone of immediate perception is limited by a height of thirty feet and a distance of not more than 100 feet to 150 feet. Beyond that distance objects are conventionally considered as being viewed from afar.

individual buildings take their place in the anonymous web of urban structures.

A new visual world is being generated from these abstract forms. Rationally planned, it is a world that represents a victory over material shortcomings and symbolizes liberty, as well as the power of technology. It is a world both attractive and disturbing, for it

141

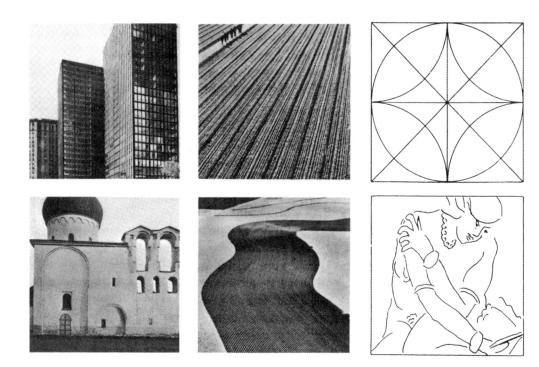

In the course of centuries architecture has produced varied and seemingly incompatible works. In all of them the millenial contradiction between the epic dimension of social reality and the lyric dimension of personal reality is manifested, between rational and irrational, geometry and design, straight line and curve.

represents human intelligence, although the individual no longer is dominant. Ornamentation also has ceased to be featured in the design of façades. This scale of sculptural and pictorial decoration is now independent of a single function or building; it can be seen in the design of roads and walkways, in small open spaces and green areas, and in the refinement of minor structures. Panoramic architecture, with its nobility and its expressive force, creates a new large-scale plasticity that is extremely different from the architecture in which scale and dimension were conceived in relation to the individual. Where one can look closely and touch with one's hands (the architecture along streets, or at the base of buildings), one senses an acute need for ornamented detail and variation.

The architect now is chiefly responsible for the

total organization of space, not only the spaces in a building but the open spaces between buildings. No longer is space interpreted mechanically, but as an organic method of architectural composition. A new world arises, a world of curved humanistic lines. Light and landscape penetrate into areas where until recently darkness and bleakness ruled. Buildings grow higher. Sun and gardens surround them on all sides. They stand free of the soil, leaving the land to man.

Rather than emphasizing the façades of buildings, contemporary architecture stresses the plastic and panoramic view and takes in the whole perceptual field. Although architecture has at its disposal an arsenal of means, it still has not fulfilled its esthetic potential. One step still must be taken before these possibilities can materialize and create a new kind of total space, before we leave behind negation and novelty and arrive at a harmonious unity of rational and emotional elements, geometry and human design.

Standardization and Multiform Construction

Will architecture be able to create a varied esthetic space, a unique environment based on the inherent standardization of mass production?

We have not reflected enough upon the very important fact that construction has now become a part of industrial production. Many consider the resulting standardization to be primitive or repressive, not corresponding to the complex nature of man. Many people view the industrialization of construction (and of other human activities also) as "the sickness of our century," for which we absolutely must find a cure.

The potentialities of mass production, however, are undeniable; the prospects for its development are unlimited. Furthermore, principles of mass production contain nothing intrinsically new; standardization and the creation of fixed types are facts of nature and always have been.

"This undeniably is one of the fundamental phe-

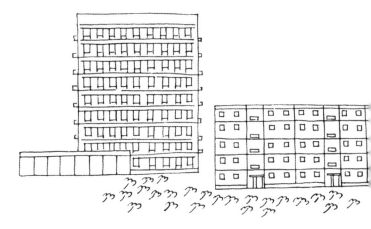

nomena of this world, which no new discovery will alter. Atomism, in its broadest meaning, or mass production as practised by nature, is the deepest scientific truth." [15]

What is new is that human beings in relatively recent times have recognized the principle of standardization and have undertaken to apply it to their own activities, particularly to the field of construction. Whatever people may say about the anonymity and monotony of contemporary architecture, every new spatial conception must work with large-scale complexes composed of repetitive building types.

Construction by industrial methods means that a whole range of architectural needs must be met by standard types of buildings that, in turn, incorporate standardized structural elements. In principle, these procedures are the appropriate result of standardized project planning. The projects thus produced, however, usually present an intolerably rigid appearance. They are the outcome of a series of dimensional and formal assumptions that leave no room for the intervention of creativity.

In these projects any required updating, or even minor changes, involves new standardized planning.

[15] J. Tjompson, **Previews of the Future** (Moscow, 1960), p. 37.

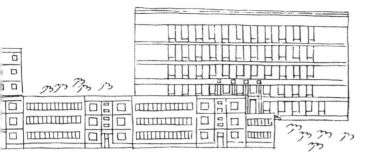

A great number of standard forms are incorporated in contemporary building, but the spatial solutions arrived at differ very little. The result is a depressing uniformity.

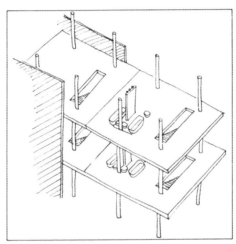

The organization grid states only the construction plan and the solution of principal functional questions for each type of structure. The façade, the shape of the building, its placing on the site and its mass are worked out creatively and specifically by the urbanist architect.

What finally results is a vast number of standardized projects that may differ in detail but are all of one general type.

The standardized project, furthermore, does not allow the planner any latitude even within prescribed limits. Because creativity is reduced to a minimum, the outcome is a depressing monotony.

Clearly, then, the ways in which buildings are standardized and assembled must be changed.

No more than general plans and the most basic functional relationships should be pre-established for a project.

145

The modular grid is a well-defined means for designating the interdependence of various spaces. Modules are designed to suit their structural and economic functions. A modular plan provides a system for planning the open and closed parts of the shell, the position of stairs, the service and access areas. On the one hand, it is able to guarantee a certain functional relationship (how the mechanical cores, elevators, and stairs will be incorporated in the structure and how the apartments will be arranged), but on the other hand, it gives the architect freedom to design within its limits. The modular grid, therefore, is the architect's indispensable tool for creating an individual composition on the basis of standardization. It allows him to arrive at diverse and flexible design solutions and to make use of both general industrialized and local craft procedures.

Variation in the Floor Plan

A building's spatial character and mass determine its floor plan. A building, as a point in space, concentrates space; as a straight line, it divides space; as a curve, it partially encloses space. The more this curve closes on itself, the more space the building encloses. In this way whole sections of open space are absorbed by the interior. The flexibility of the site plan determines building design, for it provides the rhythmic elements that compose an urban complex.

In contemporary architecture scattered buildings are being replaced by comprehensively planned projects. Even using a single standardized type of building, one can obtain variety through skillful site planning.

Variation in the Profile View

Building types differ in height, which makes their profile views important in architecture today. Such height variations will tend to transform the silhouette into a new design element of the total urban complex. This means that spatial relationships not only are important in a building's floor plans but also determine the configuration of its upper stories.

Buildings also can be made different from each other by varying their façades, that is, by differing the spatial transition from indoors to outdoors. A sharp line of demarcation can be drawn between a building's interior and exterior, but it is also possible to merge the two. This decision will determine how the façade is delineated.

The choice is independent of engineering. The architect should be entirely free in his creative inquiry. Using the grid as his basic means of planning, he can work with an inexhaustible variety of façades for one basic plan.

The possibility of variation does not mean that infinite variety is necessary. Contemporary architecture should work with a relatively small number of prototypes, each serving a specific functional purpose. In order to make genuine rather than trivial differences among them, the architect ought to be aware of essential distinctions.

We are not concerned here with the great variety of building types available for construction. If, for example, we follow the inherent austerity of contemporary architecture and the current ways of using materials, it will be difficult in practice to avoid uniformity and to obtain significant contrasts in the use of space.

In any particular instance, one must distinguish accurately among the building types available, so that architectural variations reflect true functional and technological differences. These should be clarified and used to modify the design of floor plans, façades, and profile views.

Thus the simplicity and expressive logic of each fundamental architectural conception can be manifested in different types of building. Opportunities

147

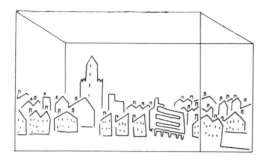

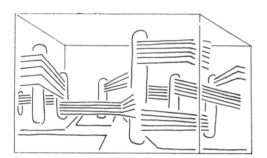

Architecture has gone beyond the traditional formal types of building units, each of which fills a relatively small space. It is working more and more with whole complex building systems. The building ceases to be a small island in oceans of unconfined space; it readily articulates that space, fills it out, and is open to it.

for variation and uniqueness in making spatial solutions can be provided through a small number of clearly distinguished basic types of building.

A critical phase in the further development of construction was reached when industrial methods began to be used in construction. At one time the resulting problems seemed insoluble. Today we are convinced that solutions exist, even if the architecture of the twentieth century has not yet been able to test them out in practice.

We have behind us a half century of experience with the new architecture. It has found its own expressive means, its own language. Why has it not managed to realize its full potential?

The best features of contemporary architecture

The plastic formation of façades no longer depends on making externally explicit the function of the bearing structure. Architecture today is free to discover an unlimited variety of formal solutions: from a neutral surface of opaque plasticity to sculptural depth created by projecting panels.

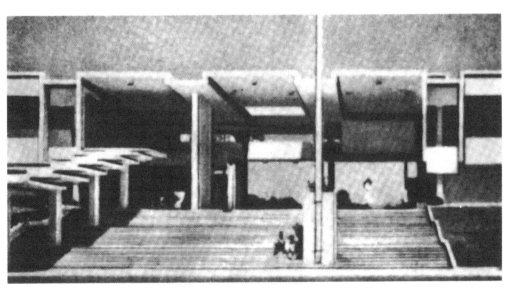

and the new qualities of architectural space can be realized only on the scale of comprehensive urban plans.

A World Belonging to All and to Each

Without co-ordinated planning neither the single prototype building nor standardized projects can be given enough flexibility in their basic characteristics to enable the architect to make creative and varied design solutions.

Up to now twentieth-century architecture has not been able to take the step from experimentation with new materials to their application on the vast scale of the new urbanism.

The desire to demonstrate his originality drives the contemporary architect in capitalist society to turn his energies away from the basic problems of mass construction. Even where the option exists for planning a relatively large and independent group of buildings, he seldom uses it to put his professional ideas into action. He must take into account the narrow interests of those who commission him (landlords, local agencies, and developers). Most binding of all, he must adapt his work to profound social inequalities.

In the typical environments created by bourgeois society, modern architecture cannot apply its principles in a logical manner. To do this it would have to establish a practical urban plan, a clear social program for the whole community, in short, interpret the individual building within its given spatial context in the contemporary city.

In substance, the contemporary architect understands space on a much broader scale than the Renaissance architect. To the latter the classical concept of the autonomous building was immutable. Yet, even today, a city's space is interpreted in this ancient way. Buildings are conceived as architectural "frames" set side by side. Space is deprived of direction, expansion takes place in a confused way, and so the urban environments gradually lose the charm and unity of the medieval town.

Up to this point we have pointed out that contemporary architecture uses present-day methods and building materials and employs universal procedures derived from all the technical and material resources of our time to arrive at functional building solutions. Actually, however, architectural procedures vary with different social systems, and so in the twentieth century there exist two architectures, one socialist and the other bourgeois. The external resemblance of their technical and expressive procedures conceals profound differences.

Social problems have always been the central concern of Soviet architecture. Architectural practice has been inspired, therefore, by the valid conviction that a socialist society creates new methods and new possibilities for solving its social problems. Yet only too often this belief has been used as a substitute for the detailed and scientific study that these problems require.

The amount of building in our country increases every year. Hence, more and more, the materials and methods of industrial production are being used in actual construction. In spite of rapid growth, however, mass building had not reached the level of efficiency of other industrial operations until recently. The quality of Soviet construction definitely lagged in comparison with the rest of the world. But great improvements have come about recently in this field: the sociospatial structure of environments has been thoroughly studied, and actual physical plans have been proposed that are in accord with the social needs of the environment. Assuming its present social basis, Western architecture in the twentieth century is not in any condition to realize a comparable program.

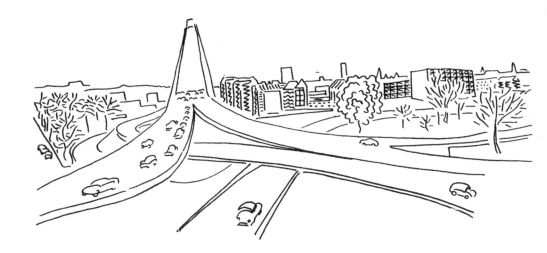

The development of an urban environment made up of standardized residential units is of paramount importance for the building program of communism.

Once a single residential building has been completed and its structure rationally worked out, it cannot be easily extended in length, width, or height. The most that can be done is to add another similar unit next to it. Similarly, the microsector, which can vary on the large or small side, cannot be extended once it has been planned because its proportions (radius and volume of services, outdoor area, etc.) are likely to be disturbed. The microsector has become, therefore, like the residential unit, a spatial entity related only to internal needs and services.

In principle, the planning of residential settlements today should be changed in the same way that the single residential unit was changed. The environment would then cease to be a chaotic agglomeration of buildings. It would become an organic whole, with all elements interrelated. An applicable type of residential unit, however, cannot be planned without also providing for a school unit. Changes of this kind in the services needed by communities must also be reflected in residential planning.

Functionalism never defined the role of single buildings in total urban space. This space, rolling over many miles, loses all traditional points of reference and cannot be perceived as a whole, appearing rather as an unending and accidental continuity of spatial events, incoherent and lacking expressive significance.

The new unit of settlement (NUS) may be compared to a living organism, having both a brain and a heart. Functional connections can be fully realized. Space in this new kind of city reflects the harmony and rationality of the social and economic structure.

This is not an outside world arbitrarily created, an alien entity seen from the windows of each house. It is a natural context directly connecting each individual cell of the society with existential purposes. Here the larger environment of nature surrounds the social organism, which is a real organism, one that includes the human collectivity. Such an environment, in short, is a place to live, where every man experiences identity as an effective member of a family, or as a member of a community in his residential unit. The new city is a world belonging to each and all, a world based upon reason and respect for the individual.

Space in the New Community

Let us discuss the unified space of the community.

If you enter a theater, for example, the space in that auditorium is a physical reality. You find its limits, and you orient yourself within them in a clearly defined way. You perceive your own presence in it, whether you are on the stage or seated in the last row. The unified space of the NUS (New Unit of Settlement) is a gigantic room under the open sky. You feel your own presence in the NUS, whether looking out the window of your apartment, leaving a residential unit, going to work, or traveling to the sociocultural center.

The simplicity and variety of the buildings and the plasticity of their planned configurations create an environmental framework in which elements do not appear arbitrarily derived and related, but are indispensable means of organizing space. The material procedures and scale of mass construction are involved directly with the vast undertaking of designing a spatial and temporal system for society.

Geometry and architectural design play a role in the harmonious framework of this unified space. The curves of natural surroundings interweave with the proportionate geometry and fundamental rhythms of this new urban architecture.

The architectural volumes contained within simple façades are integrated with the spaces that they partly enclose. They both become modulations that compose the rich sculptural qualities of the immediate environment.

Variety is achieved on the basis of a minimum number of distinctly different prototypes.

The search for architectural purity and rationality is fulfilled in plans for the NUS. Although our concepts are very general here, we have outlined schematically a system for designing each sector as part of a unified environment, including residential units with primary schools, consumer and public services, a high school community, and a focal point at a social and cultural center. Naturally, we must assume that a different course of reasoning may make us modify these plans in some respects. In fact, we have been attempting to illustrate the variations that are available to the contemporary architect within the unified spatial system of the NUS.

The solution to the problem of variety does not lie in individualizing the design of each microsector, let alone each individual building. The solution will come from designing individual compositions made up of a number of elementary prototypes. It is important, therefore, to give to each prototype building a unique configuration.

Nonetheless, whatever contrasts are stressed in the spatial design of the NUS, a common character will permeate the rhythmic ordering of volumes and surfaces. Certain functional characteristics will be strong enough to give a cohesive architectural quality and spatial unity to the whole environment. A unified space determines the role and the possibilities of any individual building (or any complex of buildings) within it, and it creates the expressive profile of the environment itself.

Tasks of the New Architecture

Functionalism has clearly shown how the spatial solution of a building is determined by its internal structure; and we add, not only by its internal structure but also by the total environment. Indeed, a building's internal structure need be considered on this design scale only to make sure that it does not contradict the rational composition and spatial unity of the entire urban community.

The future will provide new methods and set up new artistic standards. It is very likely that the city of tomorrow will hardly recall the NUS. Regardless of the differences, it will at least share certain features in common with the NUS. We hope that its esthetic qualities will express an even greater harmony of social structure and functional spatial organization.

Undeniably, the future belongs to this spirit of organic synthesis, and so we ought already to be deeply aware of it. A unified social organization, a unified technical and industrial base, and a unified artistic composition are the elements that compose our urban environment.

It is the task of architecture to speak to men in the language of form, color, light, and space. This language has an emotional impact on all people and cannot be discounted as a by-product of architectural planning. It is the authentic content of architecture.

Materials and methods of construction are not the culmination of the creative process. They represent the means, indispensable but purely preparatory. At this point, the professional training of the architect is completed, and the new architecture begins.

Since it is impossible to define precisely the archi-

tecture of the future, it is absurd to try to guess what will be created by the imagination, talent, and individual creativity of men who may not yet be born.

We can predict only on the basis of those possibilities that architecture at the present time seems to offer for the future.

Human dimensions of architecture. The glass surfaces of residential buildings of great height rise uniformly above the green area. Everywhere, from almost any spot, one feels the severe and geometric rhythm that orients the individual in the space of NUS. These are the human proportions of the New Unit of Settlement. There is marked contrast between the geometry of construction and the picturesque variety dominating the zone of immediate perception. That is the dimension where the individual predominates. Restraint in the use of structural forms and a rich plastic variety in the ground level surfaces compose the complex whole of the unified NUS.

Pedestrian walks are cut under the buildings, and in the shadow of the bearing walls along the walks there are bodies of water. The whole includes stairs, ramps, porticoes, show windows, cafés, and open-air amphitheaters. All this produces a lively sequence of architectural and spatial impressions, a rich variety of colors, forms, and light. The individual regains the pedestrian street with its human scale, something that has been missing since the Middle Ages.

The rational construction
of technically perfect
high-rise buildings. In these
can be seen the ascetic
spirit and elegance of
faultless calculation.

159

Schools and institutions for children are scattered over the green gardens. Only the transparent envelope of a wall segregates the interior space. A step brings the individual out into snow or among flowers. Another step—and the branches of trees are interlaced above his head.

Light and green. Aesthetic variety in the unified NUS is the result not only of architectural variation. Each individual building is placed in its own world of surrounding sunlight, air, and green. The contrast between high and low elevation is another source of variety in interiors.

The apartment, as an adult's home, is raised above ground level. Sun and air enter the home from two sides at differing angles of illumination. The eye of the individual takes in the whole NUS, its center, its rational network of streets and buildings, and going beyond these limits, passes over the immense surrounding spaces until it finally rests on the distant horizon, where the outlines of mountains, woods, and land are lost in mist.

Unified spatial composition. The physical unity of NUS reflects rationality and unity in the social organism. Here beauty is the natural consequence of the harmony of functional structure. Buildings take their place within it. On a large open place fed by numerous pedestrian walks, there rises the square structure of the community center—brain and heart of NUS.

Here is the place for free relationships among free individuals to develop. This is the symbol of rational and organic structure in the new environment. Here is the center of its integral composition.

The Way to Follow
Until today the history of architecture has been a history of the planning and constructing of individual buildings. Now, for the first time, architecture ceases to confine itself to this task. To design the New Unit of Settlement it is not enough to know how to plan a building. A total unified space must be designed by using a system in which single buildings make up a variable spatial field and form a total community.

The contemporary architect inevitably confronts the problem of planning a whole spatial program in which each sequential part must realize its maximum potential through intensive utilization of the entire urban environment.

Each spatial unit or type derives from, and gives specific form to, a corresponding social function that in turn reflects a certain level of human interaction occurring at work, in daily life, or during leisure-time activities.

In architectural thinking today we find that all problems in a society are related to spatial organization. It is increasingly difficult to limit any group of problems simply to the field of construction. Today the architecture of buildings becomes part of a larger creative process, the spatial organization of society. This, in turn, is a part of the general material engineering of the new world, which will co-ordinate the utilization of resources for all urban settlements. It is not surprising, therefore, that we find common methods employed in the solution of diverse problems in spatial organization.

Conditions for spatial perception have also changed substantially. Whereas a single building was once perceived as a unique spatial composition, we are now ready to conceive a unified spatial field, which includes the entire community. The new tone and speed of life are forcing us to extend our concepts of unified space to a global scale. On that scale we visualize the nuclear configurations of NUS in organizing geographic and economic regions.

From classical architecture and painting and scientific research in physiology, psychology, and mathematics, we can begin to derive general rules of construction that are applicable to any spatial composition, and relate them to the new conditions of spatial perception. Foundations do exist for this "architecture of space," and the principles need only be put in practice. We are working with a universal art that could make beautiful everything that men produce, everything in their surroundings.

The concept of unified space changes the very basis for defining the architect's work. It gives the word "architecture" a new meaning. Nonetheless, the magnificent heritage of traditional architecture should not be cast aside. Its values remain. The methods developed by classical architecture continue to be useful within a wide range. The new theory does not undermine older methods but only defines the limits of their usefulness.

"The new science never simply rejects the old, but only transforms it, deepening and generalizing with respect to new areas of research. If new theory liquidated older standards and theories, science in general could not develop. . . . Fortunately this is not what happens." [16]

The harmonious synthesis of elements in the ancient temple and the sculptural elaboration of its volume remain fundamentals for the design of any single social building located in the midst of nature. In the sculptural variety of a narrowly circumscribed area the forms of the medieval city are revived.

The system of unified space is not a matter of arbitrary choice but a co-ordinated and standard

[16] N. Semenov, **Science Tolerates No Forms of Subjectivism**, "Nauka i Zizni" (Moscow, 1965), 4, p. 38.

procedure that modern architecture has already discovered and occasionally demonstrated in practice.

It is fair to say that functionalism played a revolutionary part in the history of architecture. In light of what has been said before, however, functionalism (despite the newness of its conceptions) is in a certain sense the crowning achievement of classical architecture. The real revolution comes with planning a unified urban environment. This would be the real and profound revolution in architecture, the beginning of a true architecture of space. What essentially characterizes this revolution is the fact that the new architecture will correspond to the social process that will consciously be reconstructing society.

NUS represents an attempt to involve the thought and imagination of the architect on a global scale, outside of which the search for the new is impossible. One must begin with a basic and scientific study of the functional structure of urban communities, then go on from there to the creation of coherent urban models, until finally one undertakes experimental construction. Only this procedure can enable us to find out today what the architectural solutions of the future will be, to study them, and even to correct them.

The difficulties that await us have not yet been defined, but the way before us lies open.

Mary Otis Stevens
Afterword

THE IDEAL COMMUNIST CITY

In 1968 *The Ideal Communist City* was translated from the original Russian version into its Italian text (*Idee per la Città Communista*) and published in Milan by il Saggiatore, the firm that published Leo Pasternak's *Dr. Zhivago*. Both manuscripts had been smuggled out of the Soviet Union. So far, the Russian original of *The Ideal Communist City* has not been found.

i press, founded in 1968 by Mary Otis Stevens and Thomas F. McNulty, bought the English language rights from il Saggiatore, and commissioned Renee Neu Watkins to do the translation. A facsimile of the original edition published in 1971 by i press with George Braziller is included in this republication. Commentaries by noted urbanists and design professionals of this time add depth and a judicious perspective to the topics discussed.

The May 1970 preface to *The Ideal Communist City* by Giancarlo de Carlo merits featuring in its entirety. His comments on the major urban and architectural design concepts by the book's authors—Alexei Gutnov and fellow colleagues on the faculty of the University of Moscow in the late 1950s— continue to serve as useful guides through the book's contents.

The proposals in *The Ideal Communist City* were not based on "academic preconceptions" but on "the analysis of life in the existing Soviet society and directions of change within it." While only "sketched and presented hypothetically, they build upon the rich heritage left by Soviet architecture and urbanism in the twenties [1920s]."

In the "New Unit of Settlement," the authors advocate "world-wide urbanization," a concept that "incorporates countryside with city, conceiving both as a communication network, uniformly intense and diffused." Text and graphic components in *The Ideal Communist City* share the scale and scope of *World of Variation*, especially Part III: Architecture Beyond Cities.

A global context is common to both books, as well as their focus on future options for societies emerging from previous colonization or autocratic governance. This fortuitous convergence was why the two books were intentionally paired when initially published in the *i press series on the human environment*.

i press and THE IDEAL COMMUNIST CITY

Giancarlo de Carlo—urbanist, educator and humanist—played a vital role in the formation of i press. In charge of the 1968 Triennale in Milan, he assembled an international group of urbanists and professionals in the design disciplines to create exhibits in a Renaissance-era Sforza building now used as an exhibition hall.

György Kepes, Stevens and McNulty were among the participants selected and were assigned a long corridor for their exhibit, *The City by Night*. This exhibit featured 35mm slides of Boston at night projected on the walls and floor, while Stevens created a multimedia linear light sculpture on the ceiling in a programmed loop. When the light mural was finally installed, the senior electrical engineer for the Triennale, Castilogne, explained in English, "Look! Look! The lights are walking!"

In the months preparing for the Triennale's spring opening, Stevens and McNulty made several site visits to Milan that connected them with de Carlo and others with his objective to expand the architect/urbanist role in society beyond buildings and conventional city planning.

Later, circa 2010, when Ute Meta Bauer was founding director of the Program in Art, Culture, and Technology at MIT's School of Architecture and Planning, and Pelin Tan was a visiting fellow, they interviewed Stevens in regard to i press and its relationship to her other architectural endeavors and social activism. The resulting article entitled "The flux of human life" was published in *Domus* (issue 967, March 2013).

The objective of i press was to publish conceptual works, and so Stevens chose the Bodoni lowercase italics font for the i press logo because the calligraphy images a human being as well as serves its symbolic function—ideas, imagery, identity without personalization. It also conveys cultural overtones because the eighteenth-century designer, Giambattista Bodoni, was a noted humanist. In this context, visual/verbal language has kept the published works relevant to readers today as well as when they were originally produced.

Ute Meta Bauer, Karin G. Oen, Pelin Tan
Editors' introduction to the new edition

The republishing of *The Ideal Communist City* comes at a very interesting moment in which questions of urbanism and urbanization are visibly stressed by capitalist expansion. Furthermore, the influence of technological development in the urban sphere is still under scrutiny and a subject of debate in the twenty-first century. This book was originally produced in the late 1950s by the architecture faculty of the University of Moscow: Alexei Gutnov, A. Baburov, G. Djumenton, S. Kharitonova, I. Lezava, S. Sadovskij. It was translated from its Italian version, *Idee per la Città Communista* (Il Saggiatore, Milan, 1968), by Renee Neu Watkins and published as part of the *i press series on the human environment* in 1971 after McNulty and Stevens encountered the book and secured its English language rights while contributing to György Kepes' *City by Night* exhibition, part of the fourteenth Milan Triennale curated by the Italian architect and educator Giancarlo de Carlo in 1968. Details of the professional networks and ideological affinities connecting Gutnov, de Carlo, Stevens and McNulty are elaborated in Ana Miljački's thoughtful essay that accompanies this new edition.

The book consists of chapters that are based on the analysis and arguments of the urban environment and its organization of social production in a communist city. It is very significant to know that the preface to this original publication was written by Giancarlo de Carlo, who argued for the participation of users in design processes and was a founding member of Team 10, a group that criticized the modernist doctrine of the International Congresses of Modern Architecture (CIAM). De Carlo's preface supports the authors of the book that proposed worldwide urbanization against the typical approach of early twentieth-century city planning, organizing and adapting rural space into urban, and ideology derived from the bourgeois naturalism of the nineteenth century. The discussion echoes Henri Lefebvre's research and writings on the right to the city, and contemporary urban debates concerning citizen participation.[1] Lefebvre focuses on the differences between rural spaces and organization as a form of territoriality that was forgotten under European industrialization. In the first chapter, the authors focus on a communist town undergoing urbanization that assumes urban expansion can be organically combined with collective spaces in tandem.

The core of the book is the design program and manifestation of the communal life of a city and settlement that proposes designing spaces in relation to collective life that has open potentialities for future planning. The authors as planners and architects propose their project as the "New Unit of Settlement" (NUS), which is an urban organization that cares for the workers' everyday lives—work, common spaces and domestic areas. They are aiming to create a habitat where the future dwelling, housing and public spaces are architecturally organized in an organic synthesis in which human social interaction is the basis.

The Ideal Communist City consists of seven chapters that explore the urgencies related to social planning and the need to warn about the limitations of planning city space in accordance with communist social structure, acknowledging potential future societal constraints. These arguments address how the architect should analyze city growth and expansion in order to understand future planning needs. In the end, the authors claim that architectural thinking is closely connected to the problems of a society that can be directly related to spatial organization. New materials and engineering practices shouldn't be the core of architectural thinking. Thus, for the authors, the NUS consists of a nuclear configuration of organizing geography and economic regions. The unified space on a global scale is the main core of the spatial organization of NUS.

The republishing of the i press volume couldn't be more timely in light of the planetary paradigm in which we are dwelling. Housing, neighborhoods, and an understanding of the scales of spatial organization are vital in human survival under precarious neoliberal labor conditions and flows of human migration. Socio-spatial planning is still being questioned as one of the areas of concern of the architect as is urban knowledge as an epistemological and ontological category. Furthermore, the urban and rural dichotomy, which is very much vital in twentieth-century architecture and sociology studies, is no longer divided in many territories in our current century. The work and labor conditions—from the intercontinental freelance sector to the unstable conditions of wage labor—are now diversified, and many people do not have healthy environmental living conditions or access to public space. Though it might sound naïve that the authors believed in creating an urban life based on equality and a mobile space of adapting to social interaction, their proposal touches on many issues central to current debates of spatial organization in urban, rural and semi-urban places. Past, current and future thinking about architecture and design always needs to deal with and consider the notion of society and how planning is more than controlling urban growth. As de Carlo warns, "tomorrow should not be sacrificed to an imagined expediency of the moment." This is still valid and deserves a new look and interpretation from our current vantage point.

The Ideal Communist City was published in the *i press series on the human environment* by Mary Otis Stevens and Thomas F. McNulty as co-founders and series editors. The arguments around the planning and architecture of this type of communist urbanization put the society and the potentialities of human interaction into its core, which strongly relates to and supports Stevens and McNulty's proposals in *World of Variation*. Both twentieth-century books have something to offer in light of current debates on architecture, urbanism and ruralism in relation to multiple societies in the twenty-first century and the coming future.

This project has been the work of many, beginning with the original i press editorial team of Mary Otis Stevens and Thomas F. McNulty in collaboration with the publisher George Braziller, and the authors of the five i press books. Mary Otis Stevens and Aliza Leventhal continue to represent i press, and it has been an honor to work with them to reintroduce these books to a new generation of thinkers and readers. Mary Otis Stevens has been generous with her time, and we are grateful for her willing participation in a series of interviews to generate the new material that accompanies *World of Variation*. These two publications and the 2020 exhibition at NTU Centre for Contemporary Art Singapore were realized with the cooperation of the staff of the MIT Museum Architecture and Design Collections, including Gary Van Zante, Jennifer Tran and Jonathan Duval. James D. Graham provided valuable editorial insight in the publication's early stages. Beatriz Colomina and Mark Wigley's reflections to accompany *World of Variation* and Ana Miljački's essay in *The Ideal Communist City* provide valuable context and commentary on the books and their place in architectural discourse, then and now. Kirsten Weiss and her team at Weiss Publications have played an integral role in sharing this work with a global audience. The editors additionally thank Sophie Goltz, Kong Yin Ying, Maggie Yin, Ethel Baraona Pohl and Cesar Reyes Najera for their contributions to this republishing endeavor. Special appreciation and gratitude goes to Caroline A. Jones.

This publication is made possible with generous support from the Graham Foundation for Advanced Studies in the Fine Arts and additional support from NTU CCA Singapore, i press, the MIT School of Architecture and Planning Office of the Dean and the MIT Department of Architecture. But if not for the compassion, persistence, and resilience of Mary Otis Stevens, these two books would not have been in your hands.

1   Henri Lefebvre, *Key Writings*, ed. Stuart Elden, Elizabeth Lebas, and Eleonore Kofman (London: Bloomsbury Publishing, 2017).

Ana Miljački
Model Future in Future Modal: On The Ideal Communist City

In the flat fluorescent light of the lower level of the Gund Hall library, where once you began tracking through the call numbers and sideways-head-tilt-reading the spines, you lost the sense of what time of day it was, *The Ideal Communist City* gave off a low demanding buzz, and a glow peculiar to archival discoveries. Sometimes a book summons one. The year was 2001, the Soviet Union had been discombobulated for a decade and "the wall" had been down even longer. At that moment the general consensus about the fall of Communism was that after a long and unpleasant detour, the Eastern European and former Soviet people were finally able to get back on their path to (rebuilding) their democratic, neoliberal societies.[1] Studying architectural work and life under socialism, from within the US context seemed especially ill-fated. Myriad lessons from the Second World context were eagerly flushed out by that "infantilizing" characterization of a series of Velvet (and a few televised) Revolutions as "revolutions in reverse."[2] But as I write now, critiques have accumulated of that widespread understanding of the events of 1989 and the early 1990s as the entire geopolitical region's final, or inevitable, "return" to capitalism.[3] As we collectively begin to comprehend the scale of planetary exhaustion of resources, loss of species, climate crisis, automation of labor, it seems imaginable that the history of socialism and its built legacies might yet contain lessons of value for our collective future and survival. At the beginning of this century, however, attempting to bridge, or find ways to fill in the Cold War epistemic divide, and given the relative book desert when it comes to the history of socialist architecture, to encounter this little book on the communist city in the library of an authoritative institution like Harvard, felt like a real score, subversive even.[4]

The Ideal Communist City was filed with a few other, mostly cloth-bound books titled in official-looking Russian Cyrillic, but it was also conceptually adjacent to other curious items in the *i press series on the human environment*, including Alexander Tzonis's *Towards a Non-Oppressive Environment* and Mary Otis Stevens and Thomas McNulty's *World of Variation*.[5] A quick catalog search intersecting the terms "environment" and "communist" will still offer it up in most libraries that have the book.

As it regularly happens in research, by the time I got to this book in the early 2000s it was decidedly out of date. It had caught my eye because of its graphic treatment of circuits and cities, full-bleed photographs of abstract compositions involving human and celestial bodies, and most importantly, a set of hand-drawn sketches towards the end, that seemed to illustrate Nikita Khruschev's famous speech delivered at the All-Union meeting of Soviet Construction Workers and Architects in December of 1954. The sketches were a clear representation of Soviet architects metabolizing through their own medium this famous speech, and its political counterpart, Khruschev's 1956 "secret speech," in which he tried to distance Soviet Socialism from Stalin. These two speeches regularly mark Soviet architecture's historiography; they are understood as singular historical breaks. They literally mark time in a way that is peculiar for the accounting of socialism, because in fact, the role of such speech-acts was peculiar for its construction, with ideas, proclamations and five-year plans preceding their implementation and interpretation, from day one of socialism's "arrival."

The Ideal Communist City had, in fact, always been anachronistic in a way that also perhaps makes it permanently prospective. Khrushchev's speeches did not result in a swift transformation of the field as the usual shortcuts would have it, but in a scramble to figure out who and how would now fix the values that governed it: transform curricula, establish institutes that would dedicate themselves to standardization and its industrial delivery, write histories such that the work of those who had already once had to trade their avant-garde hats for socialist realism—and had to convince themselves of the validity of what they were doing—would not be canceled wholesale, but also work for creating space for experiments. Some forms of "thaw" were indeed seized in that moment. Against that backdrop of professional scramble, including gaps in which one could experiment for a bit, and as historian Masha Panteleyeva suggested, investment in new cadres as well as in the youth as a social category, a group of students at the Moscow Institute of Architecture (MArhI) produced their collective diploma work in 1960.[6] It was the first such (collective) work in the history of the school, and it was directly supported by the school's director Ivan Nikolaev, for its signals of the "revolutionary spirit," its nods to an earlier era's experiments—now in the hands of the new generation. Already in their diploma, this collective of students led by Alexei Gutnov proposed the New Unit of Settlement (NUS) as the unit of urbanization that would support a community of about 100,000 inhabitants. The goal, as they would suggest later, was to produce a continuous unified global environment based on scientific research of required (and optimal) social and functional relations. The number of 100,000 was offered as the magical scale of social relations—a large enough group of individuals to provide enough variation while small enough to ensure intimacy in the social fabric. They were imagining a distributed network that included some programmatic and formal variation by design, that was communicative, or cybernetically conceived, and, of course, communist in character.

The work was published first in 1960 in the ideologically influential journal *Komsomolskaya Pravda*, the official imprint of the Central Committee of the Komsomol (the youth party organization).[7] This entry was politically strategic, as it helped frame the NER network and its work as exemplary in its adherence to communist ideology, as a vision produced by and as performance of a model collective. Several years later, now occupying different positions in the field but still also operating as an unofficial group, Alexei Gutnov, Andrei Baburov, Georgi Dumenton, Zoya Kharitonova, Ilya Lezhava and Stanislav Sadovsky published their experimental research as *Novyi Element Rasseleniya: na puti k novomu gorodu* (Moscow: Stroiizdat, 1966).

There it was—the first version of the body of work produced by NER: the acronym derived from the work's Russian title. In it, they made population predictions and imagined automation and technological advancements that would allow agriculture to be equally widespread as industry and no longer tied to specific climatic or geological constraints. Despite their insistence on the scientific basis of their proposal, much of it transmits as a peculiar Second World architectural and urban science fiction whose key ideological premise was that indeed in this society where work will be reduced, evenly distributed and compensated for, there would be more time for leisure, creative production and socialization. The book has been described as "a success in the Soviet Union," in part for its popular-science orientation.[8] The scale of operation envisioned by NER's blueprint matched the visions produced in the local 1920s de-urbanist and urbanist debates. It matched Khrushchev's ambitious plans to plow the "virgin lands" of Siberia, but it also teetered on the edge between earnest ambition and absurdity, a kind of vision and work whose translation from its local context to Western discourse at the time would have been as treacherous as it was enticing.[9]

Gutnov had made some connections in the West, most importantly to members of Team 10 and the Italian architect Giancarlo de Carlo, who sent him an invitation to the upcoming Team 10 meeting in Urbino. Unable to travel, Gutnov sent the book in his stead. Panteleyeva reports de Carlo responding that although he could not understand the Russian text of the book he found the project kindred, insofar is it could be transmitted through images alone.[10] He arranged for an Italian translation of the book, which he endorsed with an introduction. Like all foreign translations of works by Soviet architects at this time, the publication of *Idee per la Città Communista* in 1968 was approved by the Soviet authorities.

In his role as the curator of the Milan Triennale in 1968, Giancarlo de Carlo invited NER to present their *Ideal Communist City* project and research. They were granted permission to do so and were even supported by the Soviet Union of Architects in an unprecedented move that allowed the architects to present themselves and their own work without the large state apparatus of selection and message crafting that was typically involved. With a short amount of time to produce the exhibition, they enlarged their team by inviting a few younger architects to join the original crew. De Carlo's Triennale, titled *The Large Numbers*, included a few presenters from Second World countries with links to his Team 10 network. NER's project faced off against Archigram. A team of architects from Boston whom de Carlo had met while teaching at MIT, Mary Otis Stevens and Thomas McNulty, credited along with György Kepes, featured their installation *City by Night*. At the time, Stevens and McNulty were in the planning stages of their *i press series on the human environment* with George Braziller.[11]

In 1971, *The Ideal Communist City*, now in English, and again with an introduction by de Carlo was among i press's first printed books. It had been nearly a decade and a half in the making. Khruschev had been replaced by Leonid Brezhnev at the head of the country and the party in the Soviet Union, while his program for fast and cheap production of standardized housing continued to be deployed at vast scales. The Brezhnev era would become known as the era of stagnation, marked by his and Warsaw Pact troops entering Prague in the summer of 1968, the same summer that Italian students protested de Carlo's Milan Triennale. In the context of the politically fraught Triennale, the social imagination of *The Ideal Communist City* may have spoken to the students more authentically than the more well-known figures of the Western European architectural scene (including Alison and Peter Smithson, Archigram or de Carlo himself).

The Ideal Communist City included graphic signals of the late 1960s architectural "humanism" (including a small image of Vitruvius's man included in a key diagram), postwar European ideas about formal "synthesis," as well as openness to architectural solutions within the sprawling urban diagrams. In its Italian and English versions, de Carlo could now measure those images against the theoretical proposals that accompanied them, and he offered it to readers as a work of global importance, as well as a work that envisioned a kind of world-city, world-wide urbanization based in "'revolutionary tradition,' to serve as an example to future-oriented planning." The book, at least in its English translation, is written overwhelmingly in a peculiar future modal: the demanding and yet noncommittal "should" dominates its language. This is not the future modal we encounter when being taught the canon, but a much stranger and less stable one that accompanies the act of translating utopian ideas into practice. As the authors describe the process of urbanization and the versatility of their new unit of settlement, which "could" be implemented in a variety of geographic and urban situations including agricultural land, small or large cities, they also paint the world in which their NER system modifies the entire planetary environment, achieving thus an even spread of this world-city, and, also, of communism. Critics in the US either dismissed the references to the "revolutionary lineage" invoked by de Carlo, or the whole book and its theoretical effort.[12] In response to Kenneth Frampton's vehement critique of the latter variety, Mary Otis Stevens attempted to clarify the i press's effort to present to the American audiences voices and "conditions as they exist in our own and in other societies."[13] Her own openness to this work was in part contained in the framing and the point of view presented in her and McNulty's i press book, *World of Variation*. Hoping to expose American architecture culture to many languages and modes of thinking, to a kind of polyphony of possibilities and worldviews, enabled this peculiar book—both in its context and beyond, both in its time and in ours—and its future modal offerings to make a mark, simply by existing on our library shelves and asking for attention. Perhaps no one was meant to be convinced of all the "shoulds" it propounded, but it still has the capacity to keep the door open for some important "what-ifs."

Reading it now, just like reading it in the 1970s, is a form of training in seeing beyond where we are.

Boston, 2021

1   See Francis Fukuyama, *The End of History and the Last Man* (New York: Harper Collins, 1993), or Jürgen Habermas, "What Does Socialism Mean Today? The Rectifying Revolution and the Need for New Thinking on the Left," *New Left Review* 183 (September/October 1990): 3–21.

2   See Boris Buden, *Zona Prelaska: O kraju Postkomunizma* (Belgrade: Fabrika Knjiga, 2012), and "Children of Postcommunism," *Radical Philosophy* 159 (January/February 2010): 18–25. In both of these texts, Buden characterizes the way that Western thinkers saw 1989 as a "revolution in reverse," which he finds particularly problematic as it happens precisely at the moment when people of Eastern Europe were finding and acting upon their collective, historical consciousness.

3   Buden, *Zona Prelaska: O kraju Postkomunizma*.

4   Anthropologist Katherine Verdery theorized the discursive orders that accompanied the Cold War political order as a particular kind of Cold War epistemology in *What Was Socialism, and What Comes Next?* (Princeton, NJ: Princeton University Press, 1996).

5   A few more books were planned by the series editors than actually got printed, but the ones that are available include Mary Otis Stevens and Thomas McNulty, *World of Variation* (New York: an i press book, George Braziller, 1970), Gutnov et al., *The Ideal Communist City* (New York: an i press book, George Braziller, 1971), Alexander Tzonis, *Towards a Non-Oppressive Environment* (New York: an i press book, George Braziller, 1972).

6   See Masha Panteleyeva's dissertation presented at Princeton University in 2018, "Re-Forming the Socialist City: Form and Image in the Work of The Soviet Experimental Group NER, 1960-1970."

7   Panteleyeva, Chapter 1: Networks and Images, in "Re-Forming the Socialist City."

8   Panteleyeva.

9   The expansive scale governing NER's vision for urbanization has recently landed it among other similarly scaled ideas, in Hashim Sarkis and Roi Salgueiro, *The World as an Architectural Project* (Cambridge, MA: The MIT Press, 2019).

10   Panteleyeva, Chapter 1: Networks and Images, in "Re-Forming the Socialist City."

11   I have been lucky to have been able to interview Mary Otis Stevens in the summer of 2021 about the i press and its publication of *The Ideal Communist City*, as well as George Braziller a decade and a half ago. Otis Stevens spoke about her and McNulty's acquaintance of de Carlo.

12   Asa Briggs, review of *The Ideal Communist City*, *Technology and Culture* 12, no. 4 (October 1971): 676.

13   Kenneth Frampton, "The Ideal Communist City: Review," *Architectural Forum* 3 (1972): 13, and Mary Otis Stevens, "A Clarification," *Architectural Forum* 5 (1972): 12.

Contributors' Biographies

MARY OTIS STEVENS

Mary Otis Stevens, born in New York City in 1928, grew up in a rural upstate farming community where she experienced the sufferings and social injustices of the Depression years and formed her societal ideas. Influenced also by Buckminster Fuller, a family friend, Stevens early on began to think and act globally.

After graduating from Smith College with a BA degree in philosophy and art history, she gravitated to architecture, inspired by her visits to Europe's cultural centers, especially Paris. Entering MIT's architectural program in 1953, Stevens accelerated her course load to graduate in the class of 1956 with a BArch degree, allowing her to practice that profession. Always resisting straight lines as contradictory to life's flow, Stevens developed her curvilinear style in architectural projects.

While at MIT, Stevens met Thomas F. McNulty, who studied with Alvar Aalto and graduated with an MArch degree, class of 1949. He was immediately made a member of the faculty. Finding that they shared many views on both theory and practice, they teamed up in 1958 to form Thomas McNulty Architects, committed to new ways to practice and communicate their conceptual explorations.

That led them in 1965 to embody their view that architecture is "the design of human movement" on a pastoral site in Lincoln, Massachusetts, a Boston suburb. The Lincoln house was never a "house." The two undulating asymmetric poured concrete walls enclosed an open interior where only the bathrooms and kitchen were in fixed locations. Otherwise, it was a continuum allowing the inhabitants to identify living spaces and change them according to their particular requirements. This communal

environment became increasingly resented by the townspeople, especially after all the worldwide attention and press coverage it received. After thirteen years, Stevens and McNulty sold the property to Sarah Caldwell, the noted founder and director of Boston Opera. She lived there for another thirteen years before selling it to a buyer who immediately blew it up and built a traditional New England residence on its ruins.

In 1968, Stevens and McNulty collaborated with György Kepes, founder and director of the MIT Center for Advanced Visual Studies, on *The City by Night* exhibit for that year's Triennale in Milan. During their site visits overseeing the installation, Stevens and McNulty took advantage of the opportunity to reconnect with their European colleagues, among them Giancarlo de Carlo, the Triennale's organizer. The outcome was the founding of i press, in association with the New York publisher George Braziller. In five years, they published five books. The first two, *World of Variation* by Mary Otis Stevens and Thomas McNulty, and *The Ideal Communist City* by Alexei Gutnov and colleagues at the University of Moscow, were intentionally paired.

Ending her partnership with Thomas McNulty in the early 1970s, Stevens returned to her quest for an American architecture that expresses its cultural roots. That led to her receiving two successive fellowships from the National Endowment for the Arts on "Vernacular Traditions in American Architecture." At the same time, Stevens began her involvement with the Boston Architectural Center (BAC), a non-profit night school providing a professional curriculum to students of any age, gender or background working by day in local architectural offices. Consequently, the BAC depended on a volunteer faculty. Many were also on the faculties of traditional architectural schools like Harvard and MIT.

UTE META BAUER

Ute Meta Bauer has since 2013 served as a professor, School of Art, Design and Media, Nanyang Technological University, Singapore, and as founding director of the NTU Centre for Contemporary Art Singapore (NTU CCA). From 2005 to 2013, she was an associate professor at the School of Architecture and Planning, Massachusetts Institute of Technology (MIT), where she was the founding director of the Program in Art, Culture and Technology (2009–12). For more than three decades, Bauer has been a curator/co-curator of exhibitions and presentations, connecting contemporary art, film, video and sound through transdisciplinary formats, including documenta 11 (Kassel, 2001–02), the 3rd berlin biennale for contemporary art (2004) and the US Pavilion for the 56th Venice Biennale (2015), presenting artist Joan Jonas. She is a curator for the Singapore Pavilion, 59th Venice Biennale (2022), featuring artist Shubigi Rao, and a co-curator for the 17th Istanbul Biennale (2022) alongside David Teh and Amar Kanwar. She was an editor of *Afterall: A Journal of Art, Context and Enquiry* (2018–21). She recently edited *Climates.Habitats.Environments.* (2022), co-published by the MIT Press and NTU CCA Singapore.

ANA MILJAČKI

Ana Miljački is a critic, curator and professor of architecture at Massachusetts Institute of Technology (MIT), where she teaches history, theory and design. She co-curated the US Pavilion at the 2014 Venice Architecture Biennale with Eva Franch i Gilabert and Ashley Schafer. In 2018 Miljački launched the Critical Broadcasting Lab at MIT, which engages in critical curatorial and broadcasting work, including an ongoing radio show titled "Conversations on Care." Critical Broadcasting Lab's work "Sharing Trainers" was included in the São Paulo Architecture Biennale in the fall of 2019. Miljački is the author of *The Optimum Imperative: Czech Architecture for the Socialist Lifestyle 1938–1968* (Routledge, 2017), co-editor of the *OfficeUS* series of books, guest editor of *Praxis 14*: "True Stories," the editor of *Terms of Appropriation: Modern and Architecture and Global Exchange* with Amanda Reeser Lawrence (Routledge, 2018), as well as of *The Under the Influence* symposium proceedings (Actar, 2019).

KARIN G. OEN

Karin G. Oen is a principal research fellow at the Centre for Asian Art and Design, Nanyang Technological University School of Art, Design and Media (NTU ADM), and was recently deputy director, curatorial programmes for NTU Centre for Contemporary Art Singapore. Prior to that, she was associate curator of contemporary art at the Asian Art Museum in San Francisco. Oen holds a PhD in history, theory and criticism of art and architecture from the Massachusetts Institute of Technology, an MA in modern art history, connoisseurship and art-market history from Christie's Education and a BA with honors in urban studies from Stanford University. Engaged with the intersection of art, technology and culture, Oen is a global modernist whose curatorial practice spans the art and architecture from the nineteenth through twenty-first centuries.

PELIN TAN

Pelin Tan is a sociologist and art historian. She is the sixth recipient of the Keith Haring Art and Activism Award. Currently, she is a professor in the Film Department at Batman University Turkey, a senior research fellow at the Center for the Arts, Design and Social Research, Inc. in Boston and a research fellow at the Architecture Faculty of Thessaly University, Greece (2020–26). She is the lead author of the "Cities" report of the International Panel of Social Progress (Cambridge University Press, 2018). Tan participated in Chicago Architecture Biennial, 2019; Oslo Architecture Triennale, Oslo, 2016; Cyprus Pavilion, Venice Biennale of Architecture, Venice, 2016; Istanbul Biennial, Istanbul, 2015 and 2007; Biennale de Montréal, Montréal, 2014; and Lisbon Architecture Triennale, Lisbon, 2013. Tan is a guest curator of MAAT Lisbon in 2022 and co-curator of Urgent Pedagogies by IASPIS Stockholm. Tan collaborates with artist Anton Vidokle on essay films on the future society, and received the short film award by the Sharjah Art Foundation (AUB, 2020). She has written for publications including: *Designing Modernity Architecture in the Arab World 1945–1973* (Jovis, 2022); *Radical Pedagogies* (MIT Press, 2022); *Towards a Critical Architecture* (Spector Books, 2019); *Radical Geography Notebooks* (Athens, 2017); *Re-Production of Social Architecture* (Routledge, 2016); *The Tradition of Oskar Hansen* (Sternberg Press, 2014); *Urgent Architectural Theories* (GSAPP Books, Columbia University, NY, 2015); *Climates: Architecture and The Planetary Imaginary* (GSAPP Books & Lars Muller Publication, 2016) and *Swamps and the New Imagination* (MIT Press, 2023).

Acknowledgments

The editors wish to acknowledge the many individuals and institutions that have contributed to and supported this republication project over many years.

The original i press editors and publishers:
Thomas F. McNulty
Mary Otis Stevens
George Braziller

Current i press directors:
Mary Otis Stevens
Aliza Leventhal

The staff of the MIT Museum Architecture and Design Collections:
Gary Van Zante
Jennifer Tran
Jonathan Duval

Contributor:
Ana Miljački

Supporters and advisors:
Caroline A. Jones
James D. Graham
Ethel Baraona Pohl
Cesar Reyes Najera

NTU Centre for Contemporary Art Singapore staff:
Sophie Goltz
Maggie Yin
Kong Yin Ying
Megan Chua

This publication is made possible with the generous support of the Graham Foundation for Advanced Studies in the Fine Arts.

For additional support and donations, we thank:
NTU Centre for Contemporary Art Singapore
i press
MIT School of Architecture and Planning Office of the Dean
MIT Department of Architecture